# THE INCOME TAX: HOW PROGRESSIVE SHOULD IT BE?

Charles O. Galvin
and
Boris I. Bittker

*Published by*

American Enterprise Institute
for Public Policy Research

Taxation issues make most public policy problems seem like child's play. They bring out the most visceral of political consequences facing a public official. Almost everyone agrees on the need for tax reform: the internal revenue code should be simplified; loopholes should be closed; taxes should be equitable. After these aims, however, agreement disappears. Taxes hit each of us in the pocketbook. To a certain extent, they influence how the economy operates. Business decisions must take the tax impact into consideration.

1969 is the year of the "taxpayer revolt," and the Congress has undertaken the biggest tax reform in years.

In this Rational Debate book, *The Income Tax: How Progressive Should It Be?*, Dean Charles O. Galvin of the Southern Methodist University Law School opts for a truly major tax reform. A highly respected authority on tax law, Dean Galvin proposes a flat rate of taxation on a greatly broadened tax base. His proposal is not a simplistic one off the top of his head. Dean Galvin is Chairman of the American Bar Association Committee on Substantive Tax Reform, an arm of the Section of Taxation. He has been studying tax reform for several years under the ABA Project.

Dean Galvin seeks a neutral tax system that doesn't allocate resources one way or another, leaving it to conventional economic factors or free choice as to what society wants to do with its money. There would be no tax concessions to shape public policy. There would need be no consideration of tax effect in business or personal decisions.

Taking another view in this book is another equally renowned tax expert, who enjoys the same impeccable reputation in tax circles. He is Boris I. Bittker, Southmayd Professor of Law at Yale University, where he specializes in taxation law. Like Dean Galvin, Dr. Bittker has served on the Advisory Group of the Commissioner of Internal Revenue, and has written extensively on tax policy.

This book is the verbatim report of the debate sponsored by the American Enterprise Institute between Dean Galvin and Dr. Bittker. Each expert presented a paper before the seminar, which included approximately 40 tax attorneys, economists, government officials, and newsmen. The seminar questioned both debaters in separate sessions, and again in the final confrontation.

The debate tends to revolve around Dean Galvin's flat rate proposal. Professor Bittker applauds the need for reform, but believes that the flat rate for all likely would create more problems than it would solve. He supports a progressive rate structure, arguing that middle and upper income groups are not discriminated against now in the federal tax structure. They get more out of government expenditures than low income groups, in his opinion, welfare and other government payments to the poor notwithstanding. Dr. Bittker believes the progressive system is probably fairer than any flat rate proposal, including Dean Galvin's. The Yale professor contends the progressive structure only mitigates the tax advantages of the wealthy. In fact, he adds, the principle of progression is nearly a dead letter now when the tax burden of different income groups is related to the value of benefits they receive from public expenditures. Quoting another tax scholar, Professor

Bittker says most attempts to get more taxes from the wealthy is "dipping into great incomes with a sieve."

Professor Bittker favors what he feels is a more realistic progression. He suggests the creation of three or four income brackets above a minimum standard. Tax rates in each of the higher brackets would be increased progressively. Dean Galvin agrees on the desirability of giving a break to those with substandard incomes. He cranks a negative income tax into his flat rate plan.

In defending his proposal, Dean Galvin referred to a recent study for the Tax Foundation, which indicated a 13 percent flat rate would raise the same amount of money that the present system now does. Base broadening, of course, is the key to the success of a flat rate. So Dean Galvin suggests these principles in broadening the income tax base:

(1) Recognize for tax purposes the appreciation or depreciation of property values each year; (2) include in the tax base the value of property ownership, such as a home, to put the homeowner on the same tax base as a renter; (3) include special services and transfer payments from government and other agencies in the tax base; social security payments, for example, would be taxed on the same basis as annuities; (4) tax gifts, bequests, devises and inheritances as income to the individual; eliminate gift and estate taxes; (5) disallow personal expenditures as exemptions. In addition, Dean Galvin would tax earnings only once. Corporate income, for example, would be taxed at either the corporate or shareholder level, but not twice as at present.

Dean Galvin has a special complaint about the present discrimination against taxpayers who provide services.

"In the last third of the twentieth century, talents and skills are going to be our basis for survival," he comments. "The astrophysicist, the theoretical mathematician, the heart transplant surgeon, the professional sportsman who entertains us in our greater leisure, the countless other service performers in a highly technological society will be the mainstay of our civilization. That these same people, the service providers, should be in a disadvantaged position in relation to capital providers is unthinkable in any projections of sound taxation and fiscal policy."

Professor Bittker isn't impressed with the Galvin proposal as a means of simplifying the federal income tax. He sees great complexities in figuring out the broadened tax base. ". . . the inclusion of large amounts of noncash income in the tax base will, on the one hand, introduce a flood of new complexities, and on the other, stimulate an almost irresistible movement for 'tax relief.' "

He also doubted that a simplified tax would reduce the time spent by lawyers for "sterile" tax planning. Dean Galvin had proposed direct subsidies rather than the tax credits to influence specific public aims. Professor Bittker sees no reason to believe the "Commerce Department's regulations for expenditures of public funds will be less complex than the internal revenue service's rules for granting so-called 'tax expenditures.' "

# THE INCOME TAX: HOW PROGRESSIVE SHOULD IT BE?

*Second in the third series of Rational Debate Seminars sponsored by the American Enterprise Institute held at The Madison Hotel Washington, D.C.*

# THE INCOME TAX: HOW PROGRESSIVE SHOULD IT BE?

Charles O. Galvin
Boris I. Bittker

RATIONAL DEBATE SEMINARS

American Enterprise Institute
for Public Policy Research
Washington, D.C.

Second Printing, 1974

Library of Congress Catalog Card Number 73-87107

## FOREWORD

This is a time of foreboding about a taxpayers revolt. Secretary of Treasury Joseph W. Barr warned of a growing resentment against higher taxes near the close of the Johnson Administration. In the first half of 1969, tax reform has been the subject of both angry and concerned rhetoric in the Congress and the press. Not only the size of the tax bite, but the inequities of it are at issue.

The American Enterprise Institute is pleased to present the views of two distinguished tax experts in the second of its Rational Debate Seminars for 1969. Both are eminent scholars widely known in the taxation field. Both have been advisers to the Internal Revenue Service.

Charles O. Galvin, Dean of the Southern Methodist University School of Law, proposes a comprehensive tax base with a flat rate of taxation. Dean Galvin is Chairman of the Committee on Substantive Tax Reform, Section of Taxation, of the American Bar Association, and he draws upon ABA research to suggest a radical change in the federal tax system.

His debate opponent is Boris I. Bittker, Southmayd

Professor of Law at Yale University. A specialist in taxation law, Dr. Bittker is reluctant to abandon the principle of progressive taxation. He dissects Dean Galvin's proposal from the standpoints of practicality and desirability.

In this book, we have rational debate at its illuminating best. The issue is critical and timely; the debaters are distinguished experts.

July 15, 1969

William J. Baroody
*President*
American Enterprise Institute

# CONTENTS

# FIRST LECTURE

# CHARLES O. GALVIN

## 1.

Last year, when Professor, now Secretary, Nutter invited Professor Bittker and me to participate in this series of rational debates, we were intrigued by the opportunity that it offered us. In a recent monograph Professor Bittker and I and Professor Richard Musgrave of Harvard and Dr. Joseph Pechman of the Brookings Institution exchanged differing views on the question of a comprehensive tax base.[1] The opportunity presented here to pursue this issue along with the companion issue of progressivity of the income tax was a challenging one. As 1968 drew to a close, however, it seemed that the subject of income tax reform was waning in significance. There appeared to be a general view on both sides of the political fence that the election of President Nixon portended a deferment for the time being of any consideration of major substantive tax reform. It is true that the outgoing Johnson Administration had been specially enjoined by the Congress in the Revenue Expenditure and Control Act of 1968 to present proposals for substantive tax reform not later than December 31, 1968; but these developments were expected to recede into the background as the Nixon

Administration gave attention to other pressing problems. Circumstances have developed otherwise, however, and tax reform is now front and center stage with both the Treasury and the Congress. All of these events add a verve and zest to this Rational Debate which we really did not anticipate when we began the preparation of our position papers.

We will try to effect a collision on issues in order to bring into the sharpest possible focus some of the basic problems facing the nation if we are to achieve a sought for, hoped for, and longed for reform in the tax laws. Since I am making the opening salvo, I want to take the opportunity to urge that we cast aside traditionalist thinking with respect to the substantive provisions of the present system and with respect to the rate structure of the present system. I ask for fresh, new approaches; let's not slavishly adhere to old ways for old time's sake but think seriously and purposefully about the kind of tax system we could have for this nation in these important and critical years that constitute the last one-third of the twentieth century. We would not be the first. The Canadians have already spent millions of dollars and countless thousands of hours of time producing the *Report on Taxation* by the Royal Commission, familiarly known as the *Carter Report*.[2] I recommend it to you as an example of the courageous, farsighted effort of one of our sister democracies coming to grips with its own tax system.

Of one thing I am certain. The monstrous complexity of the present system in this country and the inequities wrought on upper and lower income groups alike will bring the whole structure crashing down around us unless we think seriously of innovative and far-reaching changes.

2.

My remarks will relate to two major areas of concern: First, the base subject to the income tax should be substantially broadened, and, second, income should be taxed at a flat, or proportionate, rate. These two issues are, to some extent, interdependent, but they are not necessarily so. Thus, one may urge a substantially broadened tax base yet with a high degree of progressivity in the rate structure. Or one may contend for a modified income tax base, such as we now have, with a flat, or proportionate, rate. I am personally more content with a combination of a substantially broadened tax base and a flat rate, because I believe that a flat rate is more nearly achievable with a broadened tax base than with the present narrow base. Nevertheless, I am going to handle these as separate issues for purposes of our discussion.

Some numbers may assist in orienting us to the order of magnitude of our problem. National income—that is, roughly, national personal income plus undistributed corporate profits and contributions for social insurance—for the year 1968 is estimated at $713 billion.[3] National personal income is estimated at $686 billion.[4]

Income taxes for the fiscal year ending June 30, 1969, are estimated at $84.4 billion on individual incomes and $38.1 billion on corporate incomes, or a total of $122.5 billion.[5] Thus, a flat tax rate of 17 percent on national income of $713 billion would produce the same revenue—$122.5 billion—that we now garner from both individual and corporate income taxes. Please understand that I am not suggesting national income as *the* base, but it is at least a defensible base from which to make some estimates with respect to the range in which we might anticipate that a flat tax rate would be operable. In this connection, national personal income is over $300 billion more than reported individual taxable income. This is further evidence of the narrowness of the present base when contrasted with data that more nearly accurately reflect real economic income. I have recently worked on a project which demonstrates that one particular conception of a broadened tax base would permit the imposition of a flat tax rate in the range of about 13 percent to produce the same revenue collected under both the current individual and corporate income tax systems.[6]

Let me repeat. Broadening the base and establishing a proportionate rate are not necessarily interdependent. Nevertheless, there is a practical accommodation between the two. The attainment of either proposition as an objective makes the attainment of the other far more likely.

A broad-based, flat rate system would largely remove

taxes as an allocator of resources in the economy. Choices of investment, risk taking, new job opportunities, and the like would be made on the basis of traditional free market mechanisms—the balancing of costs, prices, profit margins, optimum employment of skills and talents, etc. A broad-based, flat rate system would release intellectual resources of incalculable value to the nation. Today we spend inordinate amounts of some of our nation's most effective brain power in planning the "tax angle" of business and investment undertakings; this same talent could be used in more effective employment of the economic factors of production. The freeing of lawyers, accountants, business executives, and others from the concerns of tax gamesmanship would permit the employment of these talents in fruitful productive activity of enormous proportions.

3.

Base broadening requires the adoption of a first principle, or axiom, from which we may prescind to secondary and tertiary principles of application in particular circumstances. That first principle, or axiom, is the Haig-Simons [7] definition of income which may be illustrated as follows: An individual begins life as a taxable economic unit. Assuming, for purposes of this illustration, that he has at birth no vested property rights or interests; he begins with a power of consumption of zero. Assume that throughout his lifetime he is the recipient of net accretions to his wealth; these take the form of bequests, wages, interest, dividends, transfer payments from government, appreciation in property values, etc., so that at his death he has an accumulation of wealth expressed in X dollars. Add to this amount transfers of wealth by the individual during his lifetime plus the market value of rights exercised in consumption during his lifetime, and the result is his total income. For national budget purposes, this total income must be allocated to annual accounting periods for purposes of assessment and payment of an annual income tax.

A detailed analysis of the multitude of issues that are suggested by the Haig-Simons definition is not possible within the time limits allotted here. However, some of the principal issues which would involve a substantial increase in base over the present income tax base are: *First,* the recognition of appreciation and depreciation in the values of property from year to year; *second,* the inclusion in the base of items of imputed income attributable to property ownership; *third,* the inclusion in the income base of the value of special services and transfer payments from government and other agencies; *fourth,* the recognition as income of property received as gifts, bequests devises, or inheritances; and *fifth,* the disallowance of consumption, or personal, expenditures. Let me review these issues seriatim and illustrate each of them briefly:

*First,* the recognition of appreciation and depreciation in the values of property from year to year. Present law requires an accountability for serviced-related income whether received in cash or kind. Appreciation in property values just as certainly increases the taxpayer's power of consumption as does the receipt of property for services rendered, yet under present rules the former is not recognized as income until the property is sold; the latter is recognized at its fair market value in the year of receipt. The disparity in tax treatment should be eliminated.

*Second,* the inclusion in the base of items of imputed income attributable to property ownership. If one taxpayer chooses to rent his dwelling and invests his money in income-bearing securities while another invests the same amount in a home, some factor of income should be imputed to the home owner to place him in parity with the home renter. Similar arguments can be made for other types of nonbusiness property ownership.

*Third,* the inclusion in the income base of the value of special services and transfer payments from government and other agencies. With respect to governmental services, the benefits of police and fire protection, road maintenance, and the like are generally deemed to be in proportion to the amounts paid for such services. In those cases, however, in which specific benefits are conferred upon a particular taxpayer that enhance the value of his property or relieve him of obligations he otherwise would have had to pay, then a measurable economic benefit has been realized for which the individual should account in a broad-based system. With respect to the issue of transfer payments, if an individual purchases an annuity, he is subject to tax under present rules on the receipt of periodic payments under the annuity less an allocable portion of his cost. On the other hand, transfers from government in social security payments and various forms of unemployment compensation are free of tax. In a broad-based system such disparity should be eliminated.

*Fourth,* the recognition as income of property received as gifts, bequests, devises, and inheritances. Under present rules an individual who accumulates wealth out of income must pay a tax on such income before putting it aside in investment. One receiving the same amount of wealth by gift, bequest, devise, or inheritance pays no tax on the receipt thereof. Such capital transfers should be taxable to the recipient. In such case, it would be more equitable to eliminate estate and gift taxes altogether, for they apply raggedly and unevenly depending upon the various estate planning arrangements used.

*Fifth,* the disallowance of consumption, or personal expenditures. Because of the sharp progressivity of the income tax rate structure and for other policy reasons, Congress has allowed as deductions expenditures which have no relation to the earning of income. In a broad-based, flat rate system there would not be the compelling considerations for the continuation of such deductions. In the present system in which the rate at the highest bracket reaches to 70 percent plus the surcharge, an individual with substantial medical expenses, charitable deductions, or personal casualty losses may be seriously affected by the denial of deduction. If rates could be reduced, say, to 10 percent on all income, however, then the denial of deduction of such personal items is not nearly so significant. Indeed, the imposition of tax under these circumstances is analogous to the excise taxes which are imposed without regard to the taxpayer's expenditures for consumables, investments, charity, medical expenses, or other purposes.

With a low, flat rate of tax, no income should enjoy exemption or preferential treatment, nor should any income be unduly penalized. In this latter connection, corporate income is taxed at the corporate level, and, when distributed as dividends, is taxed to the shareholders. A business in corporate form is, therefore, put at a disadvantage with other forms of business organization. Any one of several methods could be used to avoid this double-tax effect: corporate income could be attributed to shareholders in the same manner as is presently applicable to Subchapter S corporations and partnerships; corporate income could be taxed at the corporate level and dividend distributions would pass to shareholders free of tax; dividends could be made a deductible item to the corporation as is corporate interest; corporate income could be taxed at the corporate level and when distributed, the shareholder would "gross up" the dividend to include in income the tax paid at the corporate level and then claim a credit in their respective individual returns for the tax paid at the corporate level. The corporate tax is a substantial revenue producer, yet the studies to which I have referred indicate that a flat rate of about 13 percent on a broadened base, which the corporate income stream taxed only once, will produce the same revenue obtained under the corporate and individual taxes.[8]

In sum, therefore, if we really mean to achieve across-the-board fairness, then all income must be brought into the base. Each of the examples of base broadening to which I have alluded raises a host of questions about the feasibility and practicality of pushing the Haig-Simons definition to its outermost limits. Indeed, I do not advance each one of these base broadening proposals with equal vigor. They are, however, issues that must be discussed. This task will not be easy, but if we take the time and effort we spend on the present system and apply it to hard thought about new conceptions and directions, we can devise a far better tax system than we now have.

4.

A basic difficulty with the present tax system is the bias against service-related income. Any major effort at base broadening must, of course, take into account all service, or service-related, income. Of equal importance is the inclusion in the taxable base of all property income. In this last third of the twentieth century talents and skills are going to be our basis of survival. The astrophysicist, the theoretical mathematician, the heart transplant surgeon, the professional sportsman who entertains us in our greater leisure, and countless other service performers in a highly technological society will be the mainstay of our civilization. That these same people, the service providers, should be in a disadvantaged position in relation to capital providers is unthinkable in any projections of sound taxation and fiscal policy.

Under the present system we deal with items in the tax base that are identifiable, recordable, and traceable. Broadening the base will mean the keeping of accounting records and statistical data not heretofore required. With the amazing developments in data retrieval we have the capacity to carry out the much more sophisticated demands of the kind of system that I have described. What would have been impractical administratively even a few years ago becomes possible with present techniques. This is an important procedural issue, for one of the hang-ups in any discussion of major substantive changes always turns on the impracticability of record keeping, auditing, and collection. We have the means to do these chores and, in all likelihood, can do them more efficiently in a broad-based system than we do them under the complexity of the present law.

5.

The final point I wish to make on base broadening is really a transitional matter relating to both the base and the rate structure.

The argument is made that income from certain kinds of activities should be preferentially treated because of the special nature of the economic enterprise affected. That is, it is contended that even if there were no income tax at all, government subsidies would be required to induce the allocation of resources to particular lines of endeavor. If the findings of fact with respect to these issues justifies this position, then a far more effective mechanism for accomplishing the allocation will be through direct subsidy. The particular resource allocation required can be isolated from the mass, and specific formulas relating to the favored activity can be devised rather than to leave the sought-for allocation to the vagaries of a general revenue act.

### 6.

I now move to the second issue of my presentation: the flat tax rate. The Internal Revenue Code imposes a tax at rates ranging from 14 percent to 70 percent plus the surcharge enacted in 1968. Yet we all know that this rate structure is in the main so much window dressing. Every time the House Ways and Means Committee holds hearings on tax reform, there are always paraded by the dramatic statistical demonstrations of the number of people with substantial incomes—incomes measured under statutory rules, mind you, and not under the base-broadening conceptions that I have been talking about—who pay little or no tax.[9] In 1966, the latest year for which the commissioner's published statistics of income are available, in rough figures, 70 million returns were filed. Of these, 53,000, less than 1 percent, reflected adjusted gross incomes of $100,000 or more; and 218,000, about .3 percent, reflected adjusted gross incomes in the bracket,[10] $50,000 to $100,000. These returns reflected adjusted gross income as follows:

| Adjusted gross income bracket | Adjusted gross income |
|---|---|
| $50,000 to $100,000 | $14.4 billion |
| $100,000 and up | 10.6 billion |
| Total | $25.0 billion |

This $25 billion is about 5.3 percent of all adjusted gross income reported. The taxable income reported in these groups was:

| | |
|---|---|
| $50,000 to $100,000 | $11.8 billion |
| $100,000 and up | 8.5 billion |
| Total | $20.3 billion |

The tax collected was:

| | |
|---|---|
| $50,000 to $100,000 | $ 4.2 billion |
| $100,000 and up | 4.2 billion |
| Total | $ 8.4 billion |

Thus, the tax as a percent of adjusted gross income is about 30 percent in the bracket $50,000 to $100,000 and about 33 percent for all brackets from $50,000 up. The tax as a percent of taxable income is about 36 percent in the bracket $50,000 to $100,000 and about 41 percent in all brackets from $50,000 up.[11]

If all economic income were considered, the tax as a percent of either adjusted gross or taxable income would be even a lesser percentage. As one example, 50 percent of the net long-term capital gains in excess of short-term capital losses for these brackets, which is not presently included in taxable base, is about $4 billion.[12] If $4 billion is added to the adjusted gross income base in the brackets from $50,000 on up, the tax as a percentage of adjusted gross income would be about 28 percent and as a percentage of taxable income it would be about 33 percent. It is obvious that the progressive rate schedule bears little relationship to these effective rates. Even this does not tell the full story, however, for within these upper income groups, the disparity between taxpayers is considerable, some paying at the rates published in the tables, and others paying nothing.

## 7.

The argument most widely used for a progressive income tax is based on the principle of ability to pay, or the principcal of proportionate sacrifice.[13] The marginal utility of the 10,000th dollar for one with a $10,000 annual income is greater than the marginal utility of the 100,000th dollar for one with $100,000 annual income. Stated otherwise, the $100,000 a year man is able to pay a greater percentage of his last dollar than is the case with the last dollar of the $10,000 a year man. Because the units of marginal utility are of greater value in the lower brackets and lesser value in the higher brackets, the total utility sacrifice may be stated as equal.

In a small, compact homogeneous society in which there are relatively few productive and service functions, the theory of ability to pay, or proportionate sacrifice, may be a defensible tax policy. It is not in the United States. Who is to say that a dollar which a member of an upper income group spends for investment or consumption is worth more or less than the dollar which a member of a lower-income group spends for the same purpose? By what criteria are these value judgments to be made? Who is to say what the curve of progressivity should be? The mere statement of the question calls for, and finds lacking, any rational response. Even in the middle income brackets at the same levels of income, the differences in tax treatment can be startling. A single man with a $25,000 salary, using the standard deduction, pays a tax for 1968 of $8,309. A married man with two children, a $20,000 salary and $5,000 of net long-term capital gain, using the standard deduction pays a tax of $4,437. Can one really say that the first taxpayer has 90 percent more ability to pay than the second taxpayer? Can one say that the greater amount of income after taxes of the second taxpayer is put to greater use for either the individual or the society than is the case with the first taxpayer?

8.

For the principle of progressivity we pay a high price in extraordinary complexity of our present system. High rates impel Congress to enact various ameliorative provisions to soften the impact of the rates. Income may be taken out of the base altogether; it may be taxed at lower rates; it may not be recognized in the year of realization but deferred to a later period. Examine the revenue acts and technical amendments of the last decade, and almost every provision is either designed to provide relief from so-called unintended hardships resulting from the raw application of the rates to a particular quantum of income or is designed to close loopholes or prevent unintended benefits resulting from earlier legislation which in its turn was intended to provide relief. If this tinkering from session to session continues, the abstruseness and complexity of the income tax will cause the self-assessment system to collapse. The statement made in recent weeks of the danger of a taxpayer revolt is not an idle threat. The present system permits those in the upper brackets to employ able advisers to avoid legitimately the full impact of the system. Family trusts, multiple corporations, private foundations, various tax-sheltered investments, when arranged and maneuvered by competent advisers, can remove large chunks of income from the full force of the rates. Because the present system is so complex to administer, those in the lowest brackets can avoid the tax largely because of the fact that a beleagured tax administration just does not have time for so-called "small fry." For example, a casual worker, with respect to whom there may be no tax withholding, can in these times hire out his services by sunlight and by moonlight on an independent contract basis and garner a quite respectable accumulation of fees, commissions, tips, gratuities, profits on small jobs, and the like, fail to report most of it, and go undetected and free of penalty. The result is that in the broad middle group the taxpayers will more likely pay a higher percentage of their real incomes in taxes than will those in the group at either end. The middle group is generally the service performing group—executives, professionals of all kinds, salesmen, commission merchants, brokers, manufacturers' representatives and the like, the fellow next door, across the street, and down the block, whose principal source of revenue is ordinary income, not subject to shelter, nonrecognition, deferment, treatment as capital gain, or the like.

I have already alluded to the complexity in the system wrought by progressivity. A proportionate tax rate would discourage the elaborate devices for shifting income between and among entities and forward to different time periods. If all income were taxed proportionately, there would be less inducement for income splitting among family members and between family members and various family-controlled entities. Nor would the considerations for income deferral be nearly so compelling. If the tax on income in the present period is the same as that in a later period, it makes far less serious the problem of income timing; only the interest factor on the use of money by the taxpayer or the government is at issue.

Progressivity thwarts the maximum productivity of goods and services of which our society is capable. The present system tends to prostitute the talents of our most capable citizens. A skilled neurosurgeon cannot devote all his skill to his specialty; he is compelled to deflect his energies and time of concentration to investments in which he can shelter some of his professional income; the talented executive, tied to a particular company with tax-sheltered, qualified or restricted stock options, is deterred from going into the open market where his talents might be used more productively. Only the gathering of empirical data and compiling of extensive social statistics would demonstrate the extent of the consequent diminution in productivity. Nevertheless, we all know from common experience that these things do happen; they are deleterious to the individual's best performance and cause a drag on the economy.

Progressivity leads to a distortion of the effect of certain deductions. A man with two children whose income at the margin is in the 20 percent bracket gains the benefit of a tax saving of 20 percent x 2 exemptions, or 20 percent of $1,200, or $240, but one whose income at the margin is in the 70 percent bracket would, under the same circumstances, save 70 percent x $1,200, or $840. The purpose of the exemption deduction is to set some minimum amount of income per dependent as free of tax, but the low-bracket taxpayer, for whom the deduction is of relatively greater significance, receives a benefit of less than one-third of that of the high-bracket taxpayer.

9.

One objection to a proportionate, or flat rate, is that the concentrations of wealth of the late nineteenth century would recur. Such would not at all be the case. First, under the broadened base I have urged, property and service income would be treated alike. By eliminating the present tilt against service income, therefore, the tax system would not itself encourage concentration of power in a few.

Second, as I have already said, we are not taxing even now nearly as progressively as we say we are. Therefore, an outright recognition of proportionality would recognize realities as they are and not as the tax tables represent them to be.

Third, the move to sharp progressivity was made in the thirties. At that time we were in deep economic trouble. We had to use the income tax to redistribute wealth and to accomplish social and economic engineering. In these times there are other mechanisms and institutional arrangements which protect the society from undue concentration of wealth. Unions are stronger, consumers are protected against inferior merchandising and false labeling; businessmen, large and small, can fend off far more effectively unfair competition and unfair trade practices. Social security, unemployment insurance, private pensions, the increase in investment in insurance and annuities—all tend to level the peaks and valleys of the economic cycle and tend to prevent concentration of wealth or predatory monopoly. Given a highly educated and sophisticated society and a resilient, dynamic, free-market economy, we should not fear that low tax rates would be disadvantageous any more than we would fear that automation and efficiency in production techniques would cause excessively high profits. Effective communication, spirited competition, free exercise of choice for investor, producer, and consumer in a free market economy provide the greatest opportunity for the optimum utilization of all our resources.

10.

It seems to me that all of what has been just said for the flat rate applies with equal vigor if the base remains relatively narrow. We could not have a flat rate on the present base, as this would aggravate already existing inequities, but I would go along generally with some form of narrow base and a flat rate. The pressures on the Congress to offer relief legislation would be substantially lessened, the rash of institutional arrangements designed to avoid the progressive rate structure would diminish, and the strains of administration and litigation would be eased. In the vernacular of the day we would become less uptight about the system, and it would seek a level of intelligibility and administrability that would in time evolve into a broader based and more equitable system.

In short, I contend strongly for a broader base and a proportionate rate, but backed to the wall, I will hold for a flat rate, for I know that given this much, the broader base will naturally ensue.

## 11.

Now, having argued for a broad-based, low rate system of taxation, I admit to being a political and pragmatic animal. Lest my rhetoric seem too dogmatic, let me make some concessions. The first relates to the need for progressivity in the lowest brackets. If all income is subject to tax without the benefit of any personal deductions or exemptions, then the first $1 of income as to all persons becomes taxable. Administrative feasibility makes palpably clear the need for some minimum nontaxable base. Suppose one exempts the first $500 from tax and the rate thereafter is 10 percent. An individual with $500 of income pays nothing, one with $1,000 pays $50, or 5 percent of income; one with $1,500 pays $100, or 6⅔ percent; and one with $2,000 pays $150, or 7.5 percent. Therefore, some progressivity could be countenanced at the lowest bracket by the adoption of a minimum exemption. This minimum progressivity is referred to by some as a degressive tax.

Another possibility would be the establishment of a minimum subsistence allowance below which a negative income tax would be operative; that is, those below such minimum standard would receive payments to close the gap between their income and the minimum. Such payments could be substituted for some of the expenditures presently made under national antipoverty programs. The negative income tax is an important and lively subject and germane to our present debate, but we will have to take to horse on this on another day.[14]

Another concession I would make is to progressivity itself. A flat-rate, federal income tax system cannot operate unto itself; the citizen's overall tax liability includes various state and local taxes, many of which have an almost vicious regressive effect. Balancing this regressivity of local systems with a gentle graduation in the federal system is a crude way of accomplishing some kind of proportionality overall. It is unlikely that we could ever achieve a full integration and harmonization of both federal and local systems; therefore, some kind of offsetting effect in the federal structure may be necessary. The regressivity of local systems is most severe in the lowest brackets where a high percentage of income must be spent on use taxes, sales taxes, occupation taxes, and the like imposed on consumable goods and services. The basic exemption for the lower brackets, the degressive tax, or the negative income tax are suitable mechanisms for handling the problem.

12.

Louis Eisenstein in his book, *Ideologies of Taxation,* stated that it was not the question that the American people as a whole could not be made to understand the tax system; rather the concern should be that the people might understand it too well; [15] for it is then that the revolt would have its impetus.

There is an inescapable truth about this statement. We now have the capacity through new techniques of data retrieval and analysis to learn so much more about our economic system than we know now. If we were short on resources, or had a high degree of illiteracy, or had an unstable government, we might justify using the tax system as an allocator of resources, but we have an abundance of resources, a highly sophisticated society, and a stable government. We have the intellectual resources to devise a tax system which serves the nation to the best possible advantage; let's get about the job.

# SECOND LECTURE

## BORIS I. BITTKER

In discussing the subject of progression in the income tax structure I feel handicapped in three respects.

First, my qualifications: I am not an economist, with any special theoretical or empirical insights into the effect of progression on economic behavior. I am not a philosopher or moral theologian, with a professional concern for systems of justice or morality. I am not a politician or statesman, with responsibility for striking a balance among the claims of diverse groups of citizens. I am not a historian, dedicated to tracing the origin and development of human ideas, ideals, and practices. As a lawyer and teacher of law, my professional focus on federal income taxation has given me an understanding of the impact of progression on the tax structure; but when this brings me up against the moral and economic foundations of progression, I am a layman—at most, an educated layman—with no expertise or professional discipline to guide me in choosing among the conflicting claims with which this area abounds.

A second warning to be announced at the outset stems from the ambitious title of the series of which this discussion of income tax progression forms a part: Rational Debate on Current Issues in Public Policy. In a time when "non-negotiable demands" have taken the place of invitations to debate the issues of the day, and we are told that reason and rationality are either irrelevancies or hypocritical obstacles to social change, this faith in rational debate should be encouraging to the embattled academic mind. Unfortunately, as will soon be seen, I believe that in the choice of an income tax rate schedule, one cannot avoid, in the end, a decision that rests more on faith, personal preference, or fiat than on logic. I will pursue the road of rationality as far as I can trace its tracks; but for me, the final destination is not attained without wandering in the wilderness with only one's soul for guidance.

My final disclaimer results from the fact that the concept of progression has evoked an immense body of literature, characterized by a wealth of ingenious theories and a paucity of consensus among the theoreticians. In the time allotted to me, I cannot review, let alone analyze, these efforts to support or undermine progression. Fortunately, however, this task was undertaken only 17 years ago by Professors Walter J. Blum and Harry Kalven, of the University of Chicago Law School, in their painstaking examination of the intellectual history of progression, *The Uneasy Case For Progressive Taxation.*[1] Like them, I find the economic arguments, whether based on theoretical models or empirical evidence and whether concerned with stability, growth, productivity, or incentives, to be rather inconclusive; and I have no special competence for resolving the conflicting assertions of economic experts. I would like, therefore, to devote myself primarily to the question of fairness, which all commentators, even those who hold strong views about the economic impact of progression, agree are of major importance.

In this emphasis on the moral issues, I follow Blum and Kalven, who set the stage for their analysis with these introductory remarks:

> Like most people today we found the notion of progression immediately congenial. Upon early analysis the notion retained its attractiveness, but our curiosity as to the source of its appeal increased. The somewhat paradoxical character we detected in the topic is suggested by certain aspects of its literature. A surprising number of serious writers note that progression seems to be instinctively correct, although they then go on to explore it on rational grounds. More striking is the fact that the most devastating critics of the defenses for progression are almost invariably its friends. It is close to the truth to say that only those who ultimately favor progression on some ground have been its effective critics on other grounds. It is as though those who have most clearly detected the weaknesses of various lines of analysis previously offered to support progression were under a compulsion to find some new way to justify it rather than give it up. The hunch that there must be some basis on which an idea as initially attractive as progression can be justified is stubborn indeed.[2]

By way of conclusion, they sum up their quest in these words:

> The case for progression, after a long critical look, thus turns out to be stubborn but uneasy. The most distinctive and technical arguments advanced in its behalf are the weakest. It is hard to gain much comfort from the special arguments, however intricate their formulations, constructed on notions of benefit, sacrifice, ability to pay, or economic stability. The case has stronger appeal when progressive taxation is viewed as a means of reducing economic inequalities. But the case for more economic equality, when examined directly, is itself perplexing. And the perplexity is greatly magnified for those who in the quest for greater equality are unwilling to argue for radical changes in the fundamental institutions of the society.[3]

The strength of conviction in this area is amply demonstrated by the reviews of the Blum-Kalven study. John Chamberlain, in whose eyes the Sixteenth Amendment "legalizes a theft," welcomed the book for conferring "academic recognition" on "the intellectual sapping operation against the progressive principle."[4] Randolph Paul, on the other hand, asserted that the book "has confirmed rather than shaken my belief that there should be more, rather than less, progression in the American tax system."[5]

In addition to commentators like Chamberlain and Paul, both of whom found support for their contradictory conclusions in the Blum-Kalven book, there was a third group, who felt that instinct, not reason, is bound to be controlling in choosing one rate structure rather than another. This judgment was encapsulated by an anecdote in a recent comment on progression by Dan T. Smith, formerly assistant secretary of the treasury and now professor of finance, Harvard Graduate School of Business Administration. He asked three children in a one-room Montana schoolhouse to decide what would be a fair tax on a family with an income of $5,000 if a family with $2,000 of income paid a tax of $200:

> The first child said, "500 dollars," thereby showing a predisposition for proportional burdens and perhaps a desire to make use of a newly-acquired familiarity with percentages. A second child immediately disagreed, with the comment that the payment should be more than 500 dollars because "each dollar isn't so important" to the family with the larger income. A third child agreed but with the reservation that the additional tax over 500 dollars shouldn't be "too much more or they won't work so hard." Elaborate theoretical structures concerning diminishing utility and incentives and disincentives are all really refinements of the quasi-intuitive opinions of those children and may not lead to any greater certainty.[6]

Although Dan Smith and his Montana school children have left little room for rational debate, I would like to make three principal points in support of my own predilection for a progressive federal income tax rate structure.

My first point is that there is no magic in the idea of proportionality, as distinguished from progression: put another way, if the case for progression is "uneasy," so is the case for a proportional rate schedule. In Dan Smith's anecdote, the first child favored a proportional tax, *viz.*, a $500 tax on the $5,000 family, given that the $2,000 family was to pay $200. As Mr. Smith suggests, this conclusion may have reflected no more than the child's fascination with percentages or fractions, leading to a result that was arithmetically "correct," without regard to any other considerations. Perhaps, however, the use of a precise rule rather than a discretionary judgment stemmed from the same desire for certainty that led J. R. McCulloch, a century ago, to insist, in a much-quoted remark, that a departure from proportionality would be disastrous:

> The moment you abandon . . . the cardinal principle of exacting from all individuals the same proportion of their income or their property, you are at sea without rudder or compass, and there is no amount of injustice or folly you may not commit.[7]

Whether or not this conviction that proportionality is an indispensable navigational instrument was endorsed by Dan Smith's Montana schoolchild, it has found much favor among theoreticians.

I think it is fair to say that all, or nearly all, commentators on the principle of progression have assumed that it must meet the burden of proof. Conversely, they have accepted the fairness of proportionality as self-evident, needing no affirmative justification; so that proportionality is to be qualified or rejected as the governing principle only if a convincing case can be made for adopting a progressive rate structure. (Regression, however, is ordinarily rejected out-of-hand.) This acceptance of proportionality may be explicit, as in McCulloch's case, or implicit, as where persuasive objections to progression are thought to end the matter, on the unarticulated premise that proportionality needs no defense. Sometimes this bias in favor of proportionality is buttressed by the argument that progression, lacking an internal limiting principle, invites the majority to oppress the minority, and hence must be resisted at all cost as an irretrievable step on the road to tyranny. This argument, applicable to all exercises of governmental power, seems quite inconclusive to me, especially since the abuse that is feared could be accomplished, even with proportional taxation, by an unfettered use of the expenditure power to redistribute wealth.

It is also argued that progression is responsible for many complications in the income tax law and difficulties in its administration, creating a prima facie case for proportionality. To cope adequately with this point, I would need more time than is allotted to me; I will only say that, having begun my teaching career two decades ago with a conviction that most of the complexities in federal income taxation (especially problems of timing and income-splitting) were indissolubly linked to progression, I am now convinced that proportionality would not contribute very much to simplicity. Timing questions, if they involve postponement or acceleration of tax for more than a year or two, would continue to perplex us; and income-splitting issues are inevitable once we decide to allow personal exemptions and a standard deduction. They are also inevitable if progression in the income tax rate schedule is accepted as a counterweight to regressive tendencies in other taxes, an aspect of progression that is tolerated, even favored, by some of the most vigorous opponents of progression per se.[8]

In my view, therefore, the premise that a proportional tax rate is presumptively fair, with its corollary that a progressive rate is ipso facto suspect, has been an important obstacle to the process of judgment in this area, at least among theoreticians. I do not quarrel with the Blum-Kalven conclusion that the case for progression is "uneasy," in the sense that the arguments for progression are not wholly conclusive and sometimes carry implications that the advocates of progression are not willing to press their logical extremes. An equally painstaking examination of the case for a proportional rate structure, however, would in my opinion have ended with the same inconclusive verdict, *viz.*, that the case for proportionality is "uneasy." May I offer an anecdote—from Poland, not Montana—in support of this point. A Polish Communist was asked by an adversary for a definition of capitalism. "As everyone knows, it's the exploitation of man by man," was his answer. "And what is communism?" "The exact opposite, of course."

Let me expand on my heresy, *viz.*, that proportionality is no more entitled to a presumption of fairness than progression; and, conversely, that the case for proportionality must be tested by the same canons of criticism as the case for progression. What could be more clearly "proportional" than a per capita tax: one man, one dollar? Let us suppose that the amount to be raised by taxation in the United States is $200 billion, averaging out to $1,000 per person. If we pursued the principle of proportionality with sufficient enthusiasm we could raise the amount required by imposing a tax of $1,000 on every man, woman, and child, collecting this amount by leving on his or her property or wages and compelling those who could not pay to perform services to the value of $1,000. A more refined system, still adhering to the principle of proportionality, would be to exempt all persons who could not pay either in cash or in services, and divide the aggregate burden per capita among the others.

Is it not clear that such a head tax, whether crude or refined, would be instinctively rejected by almost everyone—despite its faithful adherence to the principle of proportionality? And is it not almost as clear that today's rationale for rejecting this proportional allocation of the tax burden would be that it disregarded ability to pay? And that an earlier generation of theorists would have argued that the hypothetical tax was unfair because it was not geared to the unequal benefits received from government by the taxpayers? And that a third group of commentators would argue that equality of sacrifice is the only fair principle of tax allocation, and that the head tax, though ostensibly the same for every taxpayer, actually calls for unequal sacrifices because $1,000 means more to a poor man than to a rich man? And that a fourth group would criticize the proposed head tax because it does nothing to reduce economic inequality?

Those who are familiar with the intellectual history of progression will recall that "ability to pay," "payments in accord with benefits received," "equality of sacrifice," and "reduction of inequality" are the principles that, with various refinements and in various combinations, are regularly used to support progressive tax rates. As Blum and Kalven have pointed out, if these ideas are relentlessly subjected to rigorous analysis, they have shortcomings. For example, if a progressive income tax with rates ranging from 10 to 70 percent requires a taxpayer with $10,000 of income to pay $1,000 of tax and a millionaire taxpayer to pay $700,000, we cannot know—other than by intuition—whether their "sacrifices" are equal.[9] And "ability to pay," taken as a normative standard rather than as a credit manager's assessment of collectibility, is merely another label for "sacrifice." Finally, "benefit" theory (which I will refer to again later) is similar to "sacrifice" theory in calling for interpersonal comparisons that are in the end intuitive rather than logical: who *really* knows whether the millionaire taxpayer is getting benefits from the government that are worth 700 times as much as the benefits received by the $10,000 taxpayer? As for distributive justice, if a progressive rate structure is favored as a means of reducing inequalities of income or wealth, Blum and Kalven properly point out that this indicates a dissatisfaction with the market's allocation of rewards; and they ask the advocates of progression (in a question to which I plan to return at the end of this lecture) why they do not follow the logic of this approach to the point of demanding more "radical changes in the fundamental institutions of the society." [10]

While this summary does complete justice neither to the traditional arguments in favor of progression nor to the Blum-Kalven replies, my point is that the same arguments and the same criticisms are applicable to the decision to employ an income tax rather than a head tax—or, for that matter, a tax on sales, luxuries, real property, capital gains, or inheritances—to distribute the burden of government expenditures. In short, the case for *every* tax base and *every* rate schedule is "uneasy," since interpersonal comparisons cannot be avoided.

Perhaps it will be argued that the decision-making process can consist of two steps: first, a comparison of the head tax with a proportional income tax, in which we struggle as best we can with the interpersonal comparisons; [11] and second, an independent comparison of a proportional income tax with a progressive one, in which proportionality is presumptively correct and progression is to be rejected unless an affirmative case can be made for it. My response would be that a presumption of fairness is no more appropriate in deciding whether to tax income at progressive rather than proportionate rates than in deciding whether to levy an income tax rather than a head tax. One cannot avoid interpersonal comparisons in deciding whether to levy a head tax, an income tax, a sales tax, or a property tax; and, once *that* nettle has been grasped, there is no justification for employing a presumption rather than discretion in fixing the rate schedule for whatever tax base is adopted. If, having candidly acknowledged the difficulties in making interpersonal comparisons, we prefer an income tax to a head tax on "ability to pay" or "equal sacrifice" grounds, the use of a proportional rate in no way purges our decision of any of its uncertainties.

At the risk of repetition, I would say that the maxim, "When in doubt, stick with proportionality," is no better a guide than "When in doubt, divide the tax burden on a per capita basis." The policymaker *must* exercise judgment in deciding which tax base and which tax rate is best; if he waits, like Buridan's ass, to be prodded by a presumption, he will starve.

In the hope that I have dismantled an obstacle to a fair assessment of graduated income tax rates, I would like now to offer several independent grounds for favoring a substantial degree of progression.

First, progression in the federal income tax serves to

counterbalance regressive tendencies in other federal, state, and local taxes. Even those who favor an allocation of the nationwide tax burden that is proportionate to the taxpayer's income are ordinarily prepared to accept progression in one tax structure if it serves only to counterbalance regression elsewhere.[12]

In applying this limited principle, of course, one encounters both conceptual and computational difficulties. If local property taxes are treated as though paid solely by homeowners, tenants, and consumers, this type of tax will seem more regressive than if one assumes that its burden falls partly on the owners of real estate. Conversely, if the corporate income tax is allocated wholly to shareholders, its impact will be more progressive than if it is thought to fall partly on employees and consumers.

Conclusions about the degree of actual progression in the tax system are also heavily affected by the way one defines the base against which the aggregate tax burden is calculated. It is of course familiar learning that the progressive rates of existing law apply to a less-than-comprehensive income tax base, producing the tax result that Henry Simons described as "digging deep with a sieve."[13] The popular imagination has been caught by recent Treasury studies showing that wealthy taxpayers, ostensibly subject to a marginal income tax rate of 70 percent, often pay only a modest or even trivial percentage of their "total" income—the disparity resulting from a difference between "taxable income" as defined by existing law, and "total" income as defined by the Treasury in calculating the effective rate.[14] In converting the statutory concepts of "adjusted gross income" or "taxable income" into this amended base on which the effective rate is calculated, it is customary to add the untaxed portion of long-term capital gains, exempt interest from state and municipal bonds, excess percentage depletion, and sometimes such other items as personal deductions and unrealized appreciation on property contributed to charities.

When the aggregate burden of federal, state, and local taxes is computed as a fraction of this expanded income tax base, our tax structure looks a lot less progressive than if the burden is computed against "taxable income" as defined by existing law. Moreover, if one expands the tax base still more, by adding undistributed trust and corporate income (especially if a broad concept of corporate income is substituted for corporate income as now defined), or by taking into account unrealized increases in the taxpayer's wealth (e.g., growth in the value of marketable securities, real estate, etc.), the "effective rate" of the federal income tax on wealthy taxpayers falls even more.

It seems reasonable, therefore, to conclude that the aggregate tax burden is pushed in a regressive direction by local property taxes, state and local sales taxes, federal excise and employment taxes, and the corporate income tax to the extent that it falls on consumers and employees. The only counterbalancing elements, then, are the federal personal income tax and the corporate income tax to the extent that it falls on shareholders; and the broader the income benchmark used for this calculation, the less impressive is their contribution to progression. Although some students of the national tax burden have recently asserted that its impact is progressively higher as income rises, these conclusions depend on assumptions that are, in my opinion, open to challenge, especially in regard to the definition of income.[15]

Pending re-examination of this issue on a different set of premises about the appropriate income base—and fully acknowledging that we have no all-purpose, universally-accepted definition of income (a point that I myself have recently argued with vigor)[16]—I wish here only to stress the fact that progression in the federal personal income tax is entirely consonant with the achievement of a national tax burden that is proportional to income. Indeed, given this goal, a significant degree of progression is probably indispensable. To be sure, the broader the income tax base, the less progressive a rate structure will be necessary to achieve proportionality; but if we take account of political realities, including the fact that even the minimum tax proposed in 1968 by the outgoing Treasury staff combined a less-than-comprehensive base with a modest rate structure, the advocates of overall proportionality ought to support progressive income tax rates for some years to come.

A second reason for supporting, or at least acquiescing in, progression is that it is an inevitable consequence of allowing a personal exemption in computing income tax liability. Even if we exempt no more than bare subsistence in computing taxable income, and apply a uniform rate to all income above the survival level, the effective rate on total income will start at zero and rise until it is just short of the nominal rate. Thus, a 10 percent rate on all income above the first $1,000 translates into an effective rate of zero for a taxpayer with $1,000 of total income, 5 percent for the taxpayer with $2,000 of total income, 9 percent for the taxpayer with $10,000 of total income, 9.9 percent for the taxpayer with $100,000 of total income, and so on. This type of progression, resulting solely from the allowance of a personal exemption, has special characteristics, of which the most notable is that it calls for—and permits—only two judgments: the amount to be exempted, and the total amount of revenue to be raised. Once these elements are specified, the tax rate follows automatically; there is no room in the system for comparing the $2,000 taxpayer's ability to pay or his "sacrifice" with the $100,000 taxpayer's ability to pay or his sacrifice. For McCulloch, who did not want to go to sea without a rudder or compass, this form of progression should be quite tolerable, and it would also be comforting to Dan Smith's Montana schoolchild, who could display his skill in arithmetic by deriving the proper tax rate, given the distribution of income, the amount of the exemption, and the total revenue to be raised.

The relationship between personal exemptions and the rate structure is perceptively discussed by Blum and Kalven, who point out that a personal exemption has the effect of dividing citizens into two groups: those below the exemption, who pay no income tax, and those above it, who pay something. Once this dividing line is established, it is only a short step in practice—though perhaps it is a break with theory—to establish other boundaries, distinguishing among the taxpayers who are above the exemption level. As Blum and Kalven put the point:

> The proposal of either radically high or radically low exemptions will almost certainly invite the compromise proposal to graduate rates to some degree. If the exemption is of those below the subsistence minimum, graduation will be required to soften the impact of the tax on the poor. If the exemption is set high on equality grounds, both fiscal and political considerations will again call for graduated rates to keep enough persons in the system as taxpayers. Finally, these considerations invite a suspicion, albeit rather faint, that the whole elaborate superstructure of graduated rates is but a by-product of the difficulties of handling the exemption problem.[17]

I would add only that there may well be an intermediate step, contributing to the decision to establish graduated rates once it has been decided that a personal exemption has been allowed: *viz.*, recognition that "bare subsistence" is not the only possible benchmark for a personal exemption, and that the rationale underlying the personal exemption does not lead inexorably to the division of citizens into two groups, exempt and tax-paying. One could exempt those below the subsistence level, while classifying persons above this level into two or three categories to be taxed correspondingly—all without doing irreparable harm to the theory of personal exemptions. Thus, employing the recent guidelines of the Bureau of Labor Statistics for an urban family of four, one might use personal exemptions to exempt such a family with less than $6,000 of income, tax at a low rate families in the $6,000-$9,000 bracket, impose a somewhat heavier rate on those in the $9,000-$13,000 bracket, and tax still more heavily those above the $13,000 benchmark.[18] Of course, these gradations entail the exercise of judgment, whereas a single exemption at the "subsistence" level is sometimes asserted to allow for no discretion; but whatever may be the case in a primitive society (which could not impose an income tax anyway), our concept of "subsistence" is cultural rather than physiological. The exercise of discretion, therefore, is inescapable in the selection of the dollar amount to be exempted, whether we choose to protect enough for a "subsistence," a "modest," or a "comfortable" standard of living. The range of judgment is brought home when one notes that the aggregate amount allowed to a family of four as personal exemption was about six times the per capita personal income in the 1930s, but is only about 4/5ths today.[19]

If the traditional theory of personal exemptions as a method of separating one tax-exempt class from one taxpaying class is revised to embrace two or three groups of taxpayers, the rate schedule is no longer determined automatically by the exemption level and the revenue objective. It will be necessary to compare the rate applicable to the middle group (or groups) with the rate for the top group, using "fairness," "equalitarianism," "ability to pay," "equal (or proportional) sacrifice," or a similar criterion to decide if the relationship is "right." At this point, the progression achieved as a "by-product" (to use Blum and Kalven's phrase) of personal exemptions can hardly be distinguished from garden-variety progression. Even if the exemption levels are beyond controversy, itself an unlikely hypothesis, the "spread" between the intermediate tax rate (or rates) and the top rate must rest, in the end, on an interpersonal judgment.

Another foundation for progression, in my opinion, is that economic security increases more than proportionately as we move up the income scale. It is well-known that investment income becomes an ever-increasing fraction of total income,[20] and it seems quite likely that this phenomenon would be even more pronounced if unrealized appreciation in stock, real estate, and business goodwill were taken into account. These forms of realized and unrealized income, representing either accumulated or inherited wealth, are not impaired by illness or destroyed by death; by contrast, wages, salaries, professional fees, and similar forms of earned income are much more precarious. Moreover, accumulated or inherited wealth is on the whole probably more mobile than personal skills, so that it can be more easily shifted from less profitable to more profitable pursuits as economic conditions require. When personal skills become technologically or geographically outmoded, however, it is hard for the old dogs to learn new tricks, or to accustom themselves to new masters.

Contemporary income tax theory, however, is wedded to the notion that one dollar of income is just like every other dollar of income, and that disaster will ensue if we look to the source of income in determining how it should be taxed. It is, of course, true that every dollar has the same purchasing power, and that the purveyor of wine, women, and song does not ask whether your dollar was earned by clipping bond coupons or by digging ditches. In this sense, a dollar is a dollar is a dollar. If one gives any credence to the ability-to-pay rationale, however, it is hard to disregard the source of the taxpayer's income in appraising the fairness of the tax burden imposed on him.

On the other hand, a system of different rates for different types of income—like the English schedules—has serious administrative disadvantages; and I suspect that an understandable antipathy to importing these problems into the United States tax structure accounts for the insistence by most American commentators that the source of income is totally irrelevant to the taxpayer's ability to pay. Acknowledging the difficulties that would be introduced by explicitly differentiating the tax burden by reference to the source of income, I would suggest that progression in the rate schedule is a reasonable indirect way to accomplish the same objective. To be sure, it is only a rough-and-ready way of doing so; although the proportion of unearned income probably rises fairly steadily with total income, every tax bracket contains a range of taxpayers, from those with nothing but earned income to those with nothing but investment income. If rates are graduated as an indirect way of imposing a heavier burden on unearned income, some upper-income taxpayers who derive all of their income from personal services will feel the pinch. On balance, however, I think it would be better to accept this result than to grasp either of the two polar alternatives, *viz.*, to act as though the source of income had no bearing on ability to pay taxes; or to establish a schedular system of taxing each income source separately.

To some extent, moreover, the apparent unfairness of imposing graduated rates on upper-bracket taxpayers even if they derive their income from personal services is mitigated by the fact that very high salaries usually betoken a degree of security that is comparable to the security generated by income from property. In the upper brackets, high personal earnings are often buttressed by long-term employment contracts, stock options, generous retirement plans, life insurance and other safeguards against the vicissitudes of life that are not available to taxpayers in the lower brackets.

My comments on the fairness of a graduated income tax have so far not taken account of the benefits received by the taxpayer from the public expenditures financed by him and his fellow taxpayers, and I would like now to turn to this subject in making my final point. For many years, the "benefit" theory of taxation has been moribund; indeed, Blum and Kalven asserted that its epitaph was pronounced by John Stuart Mill, who asserted:

> Government must be regarded as so pre-eminently a concern of all, that to determine who are most interested in it is of no real importance. If a person or class of persons receive so small a share of the benefit as makes it necessary to raise the question, there is something else than taxation which is amiss, and the thing to be done is to remedy the defect, instead of recognising it and making it a ground for demanding less taxes.[21]

Mill also argued that the persons who would suffer most if the protection of government were to be withdrawn would be those "who were weakest in mind or body, either by nature or by position," so that a tax system geared to the taxpayer's benefits would impose the heaviest burden on "those who are least capable of helping or defending themselves."

In asserting that the poor benefit more from government than the rich, Mill may have been contrasting the England of his day with a feudal society, on the unstated assumption that the rich (primarily great landlords) would have been powerful and independent feudal barons if "the protection of government" were withdrawn; at any rate, if this were the only alternative model, there would be some validity in his argument. It is surprising, however, that the French Revolution did not suggest another model to him, *viz.*, that "those to whom the protection of government is the most indispensable" are the lords and their ladies, not the wretched of the earth. If wealth is seen as dependent for its protection on the existence of a legal order, rather than as an attribute of man which antedates government and can be preserved by self-help, Mill's argument collapses. What good are stock certificates, or even deeds to real estate, in a society in which ownership depends on brute force?

To reject Mill on the ground that government may be as important to the rich, or even more important, than it is to the poor, however, does not carry us very far: if the tax burden is to take account of the benefit received by the taxpayer, a measuring stick is required. Is anything more than intuition available?

In answering this question, a good starting point is a recent study by Professor W. Irwin Gillespie, "Effect of Public Expenditures on the Distribution of Income," which estimates for each income level the aggregate tax burden borne by taxpayers in that bracket and the value of the benefits received by them from public expenditures.[22] By subtracting the group's benefits from its taxes, Professor Gillespie derives the "fiscal incidence" applicable to the group. To summarize his findings very roughly, he concludes that families with money income of $3,000 or under receive a net benefit from this combination of taxes and expenditures of about one-half of their "adjusted broad income" (an adjusted and expanded income base), that families with $3,000-$4,000 of money income receive a net benefit of about 20 percent of their "adjusted broad income," that families with $4,000-$10,000 of money income come out about even, and that those with $10,000 of money income or more give up about 13 percent of their adjusted broad income. Using dollar amounts rather than percentages, this means that about $18 billion is shifted from families with money income of $10,000 or more to families with $4,000 or less.

This bird's-eye view of our fiscal system suggests that the principle of progression—so much debated in Academe—is nearly a dead letter, in that families at the bottom of the economic heap are merely brought up to the poverty level, those between poverty and a modest standard of living are left alone, and those above the modest level are called upon for a relatively small contribution.

Unfortunately, Professor Gillespie's top income bracket—families with money income of $10,000 or more—is very broad, no doubt because of a paucity of data, so we do not know how he would rate the "fiscal incidence" of taxes and governmental benefits for such sub-categories as \$10,000-\$25,000, \$25,000-\$50,000, \$50,000-\$100,000, and so on. In view of the regressive nature of most state and local taxes and of federal excise and social security contributions, however, it would seem that some progression in the federal income tax would be necessary to produce even proportionality in "fiscal incidence" among these families above the \$10,000 benchmark. This need for progression would be more pronounced if the income base used to measure "fiscal incidence" were broadened to take account of unrealized appreciation in the value of the taxpayer's assets.

More important, there are obviously many ways to measure the value of the governmental benefits received by taxpayers at different income levels. Professor Gillespie has pointed this out in his study, in which he offers four alternative assumptions for the allocation of "general expenditures" (national defense, international affairs, general government control, and civilian safety, police, and prisons), *viz.*, distributing these expenditures equally among all families or proportionately to "broad income," income from capital (dividends and interest), or "disposable income" (family money income less tax payments). His computation of "fiscal incidence," as summarized earlier, is based on the second of these assumptions (allocation of general expenditures to "broad income"); he does not work out all of the alternative possibilities, except to observe that if general expenditures were allocated to investment income, there would be almost no redistribution in his highest income bracket (family money income of $10,000 or more). Such an allocation, as Professor Gillespie points out, would accord with the nineteenth century "protectionist" version of the benefit theory.

Old-fashioned or not, the idea that governmental expenditures on international affairs, national defense, and public order are of special importance to those who are moderately and well off is very appealing to me. Indeed, I would assert that the benefits of these expenditures increase progressively with income and wealth, and that families below a minimum standard of income ought to be omitted from the allocation formula. Obviously, this suggestion rests on judgment rather than rigorous proof, but this is equally true of Professor Gillespie's alternative assumptions. As I argued earlier about proportionality and progression in the income tax structure, it is misleading to think that proportionality is a priori correct and that any other principle must shoulder a special burden of proof. For me, it would be clearly more reasonable to allocate such expenditures as foreign economic aid, NATO, and the exploration of outer space to those of us who are relatively well-off than to the poor of our society, and I am almost equally sure that we will achieve greater fairness in allocating the burdens of government if we follow the same principle as to all expenditures for national defense, international affairs, and public order, and if we increase the allocation progressively as income and wealth rise.

Pursuing this analysis, I would also want to reconsider the allocation employed by Professor Gillespie for some governmental expenditures that he assigned to specific recipients. Thus, rather than allocate public expenditures for education on what Professor Gillespie calls the "straightforward" theory that the government incurs these expenditures "on behalf of one beneficiary group—the students who receive the education," [23] I would suggest that we all benefit from public education. The principle that bachelors must pay school taxes seems sensible to me, not oppressive; and I would assert that the quality of life, especially for those who are moderately well-off, is improved immensely by a widely-shared high level of literacy, university education, and culture.

I would make a similar point about expenditures for public welfare, such as low-cost housing, public assistance and the redistributive part of social security payments. Expenditures to keep people from living or dying in the streets should not, in my opinion, be allocated exclusively to the recipients of such aid; it may or may not be more blessed to give than to receive, but we all derive *some* benefit from the alleviation of human misery. When they turn their attention to charitable contributions, tax economists almost uniformly argue that these are consumption expenditures from which the donor gets what he pays for, *viz.*, personal satisfaction, undiminished by the fact that the recipients also benefit from his generosity. For the taxpayer, philanthropy by the government is of course less voluntary than his personal benefactions; this may possibly reduce, but it should not negate, the satisfaction of knowing that he lives in a decent society. If we want to discount the benefits he gets from these public expenditures to reflect his limited control over them, we can allocate them partly to the direct recipients and only the balance to the involuntarily-generous taxpayer. I would, however, assign the latter portion exclusively to those who are above a minimum standard of living, and use a progressive formula in allocating this amount within the target group.

This line of reasoning leads me to the conviction that the aggregate benefit of government expenditures is not shared by the citizenry on a per capita basis, nor even proportionately to income, but in a ratio that increases progressively with income and wealth. I would very much like to see Professor Gillespie's work extended, to embrace an alternative allocation of public expenditures along the lines I have suggested, and with his very broad top income bracket subdivided into three or four categories. If this were coupled with an adjustment of his income concept to take account of unrealized appreciation (and depreciation) in the fair market value of assets, I venture the guess that the resulting fiscal burden on upper income groups would be regressive or, at most, proportional, rather than progressive. In the end, therefore, the progressive rate schedule of today's income tax law may do no more than partially mitigate a bias both in public expenditures and in the incidence of other taxes that favors upper income taxpayers.

Finally, I favor progression as a measure to reduce economic inequality. In making this point, I am tempted simply to put it forth and make no effort to argue for it, in the conviction that one either accepts this objective or rejects it as part of his view of the good society. Assuming that argument on so basic a matter can persuade, surely nothing can be said at the end of a one-hour talk that will make a difference. As Blum and Kalven say, "The . . . subject of economic equality either may not be amenable to discussion or it may admit of infinite discussion."[24]

Mindful of the title of this series, however, I think I ought at least to comment on the Blum-Kalven observation that:

> . . . it is quite difficult to sponsor progression on the basis of economic equality without calling into question either the meaningfulness of personal responsibility or the fairness with which the market distributes rewards.[25]

This led Blum and Kalven to the related observation that it is perplexing to find progressive income tax rates advocated as a way of reducing economic inequality by persons who are "unwilling to argue for radical changes in the fundamental institutions of the society."[26]

I cannot accept the argument that advocacy of socially-prescribed constraints on economic inequality is so inconsistent with a free market that it constitutes, or should if logically pursued lead to, "radical changes in the fundamental institutions of the society." There is a one-dimensional aura about this theory that reformers should shape up or ship out, reminiscent—ironically—of the apocalyptic slogans of the New Left. It is the product, in my view, of a failure to take adequate account of two characteristics of our society.

First, the only market that can be properly regarded as a "fundamental institution" of our society is a set of socially-prescribed rules for the conduct of economic affairs, differing in many respects from the "free market" that is described in economic textbooks. Governmental agencies regulate or even prescribe the prices and terms on which many goods and services are exchanged, and in some areas the public, acting through its political institutions, determines who may engage in economic activity and how much may be produced. These constraints are so pervasive that one could turn the Blum and Kalven point around, and say that those who *object* to restrictions on the market are the radicals who are attacking the fundamental institutions of our society.

Secondly, the market is not our society's only fundamental economic institution—we have a congeries of rules and agencies that serve, sometimes directly and sometimes indirectly, to alter the distribution of wealth and income: these range from public assistance to inheritance taxation, from laws requiring parents to support their children to prohibitions on disinheriting one's wife, from free public education to compulsory service in the armed forces, and so on. It is within this framework, in which redistribution is as American as apple pie, that we must fit our decisions about the allocation of the tax burden. These decisions are bound to alter the distribution of wealth and income as determined, prior to the imposition of taxes, by the market; and I see no conflict with "the fundamental institutions of the society" in allocating the tax burden in a manner that will reduce economic inequality, rather than increase it or leave it unchanged. Such a conflict can be conjured up, to be sure, but it requires one to substitute an imaginary free market for the restricted market that our society has actually created, and then to pretend that the redistribution of income or wealth through the allocation of tax burdens, by questioning the finality of the market's distribution of rewards, is an alien intruder in a society that is otherwise innocent of this heresy. In short, our "fundamental institutions" include a less-than-free market and a set of half-way measures to reduce economic inequality, coupled with a willingness to live in a state of tension rather than to sacrifice one in order to purify the other. Progressive tax rates, in my view, fit comfortably within this form of democratic capitalism.[27]

In conclusion, then, I agree with Blum and Kalven

that the case for progressive taxation is "uneasy," but it seems no more uneasy than the case for proportionality or for preferring one tax base over another. Even those who prefer an overall proportional result are willing to accept a progressive income tax rate schedule as a corrective to regression elsewhere; and progression is inescapable if personal exemptions are employed to protect an initial layer of income. Beyond these foundations for progression, which though modest in theory may justify a significantly graduated rate schedule in practice, I have suggested that progression can be grounded as an analysis of the benefits conferred by government, as well as on a desire to reduce economic inequality.

# REBUTTALS

## BORIS I. BITTKER

I wish to make three principal points in response to Dean Galvin's presentation.

### I

Dean Galvin's case for broadening the federal income tax base and imposing a proportional tax on the expanded base—a reform proposal that would permit, he estimates, a flat rate of about 13 percent—rests very heavily, indeed almost exclusively, on the resulting elimination of complexities in planning and effectuating business and personal transactions, in determining the taxpayer's liability, and in administering the tax laws. In my opinion, he has greatly overestimated the contribution that a flat rate applied to a broadened base would make to simplification.

Confining myself to the five principal changes recommended by Dean Galvin, I see new complexities in each of them that must be offset, if we are to have a complete audit, against the complexities that they will eliminate:

1. Inclusion of unrealized appreciation and depreciation entails valuation problems which may be sub-

stantial in some areas; and if this change is accompanied by provisions for delayed payment of the tax in recognition of the inclusion of noncash income, this too will be a source of administrative and perhaps even judical complications.

Inclusion of unrealized appreciation in the tax base would conflict with the cash receipts and disbursements method of accounting, and I assume therefore that Dean Galvin would require all taxpayers to employ accrual accounting in order to present an accurate account of their economic well-being. Would a lawyer who works for five years on a client's problem and then waits two years for payment be required—in keeping with the Haig-Simons definition of income—to take the reasonable value of his work into income as the work progressed, despite the fact that collection will be delayed for many years? When I left government service some years ago and decided not to withdraw my retirement contributions from the civil service fund because the benefits that would commence 30 years later were worth much more than the lump sum I would have received in settlement, should I have reported the market value of the annuity as income? Rather than barrage you with questions of this type, I will simply assert that the inclusion of large amounts of noncash income in the tax base will, on the one hand, introduce a flood of new complexities, and, on the other, stimulate an almost irresistable movement for tax "relief."

2. The inclusion of imputed income from the ownership of property is also dependent on valuations that may be open to contests.

3. As to the value of special services and transfer payments from government and private agencies, Dean Galvin asks that we distinguish between taxable receipts from these sources and "the benefits of police and fire protection, road maintenance, and the *like*" which are "generally deemed to be in proportion to the amounts paid for such services." This modest proposal, in my view, will require some very fine distinctions to be drawn in actual practice.

4. The inclusion of gifts, as proposed by Dean Galvin, requires a distinction between amounts received as "gifts" by children (for example) and amounts received by them as "ordinary support." In applying the federal gift tax, we have sidestepped this distinction in most cases by generous exclusions and exemptions, as well as by a practice—widespread even though not sanctioned by the statute—of disregarding transfers unless they consist of cash, marketable securities, or real estate. Unless Dean Galvin proposes to carry forward these lenient rules, his reform will call for some fine distinctions between nontaxable transfers by way of support, on the one hand, and taxable gifts, on the other. If my adult children live in my home or are my guests on a trip to Europe, for example, or if I pay for the school or college education of my grandchildren, are the re-

cipients to include the value of the hospitality or the amount of tuition payments in their income?

5. Even the proposed disallowance of personal expenditures is not without its own complexities. Will a person injured in the course of his work be permitted to deduct the physician's bill as a business expense? Will I be allowed to deduct the interest on my home mortgage if I incurred or continue the debt in order to finance a business or to purchase investment securities? If my employer, or my business or professional interests, put pressure on me to contribute to the Community Chest, will the payment be deductible as a business expense? These issues are soft-pedalled today, because a personal deduction is usually available; but the distinction between personal and business expenditures would become more important with Dean Galvin's reform. I assume that if I am in an automobile accident, the damage to my car would no longer be a deductible casualty loss, under Dean Galvin's proposed elimination of personal deductions. But if I am reimbursed for the loss by my insurance company or the other driver, do I have income, in view of the consequent improvement in my personal balance sheet? If I incur hospital and doctors' bills in the accident, no medical expense deduction would be allowed; but if I collect from Blue Cross or Blue Shield, is the reimbursement to be reported as income to the extent that it exceeds the premiums paid for coverage? If I am sued by the other driver and he gets a judgment against me for $100,000, I would not

be able to deduct this loss; but if it is paid by my insurance company for me, or if I settle it for $10,000, it is discharged in bankruptcy, or barred by the running of the statute of limitations, does the resulting elimination of a $100,000 liability constitute income to be reported under Dean Galvin's proposal? Perhaps it will be said that Henry Simons would never have wished to include such items in taxable income. Perhaps not: like most economists, he viewed the world from the macro-economic heights of Mount Abstract, and wanted to leave the details to lawyers and accountants. I don't blame him, but I cannot accept the notion that his definition of income is the key to simplicity.

Another area of some importance is the treatment of corporate income. If appreciation and depreciation in corporate stock owned by the taxpayer is taken into account, there is really no need to compute corporate income, or even the business income of proprietorships and partnerships: we could simply value the assets (or stock) and add any withdrawals in the form of dividends or otherwise. But Dean Galvin's paper suggests that corporate income could be taxed either directly to the shareholders (as with Subchapter S corporations) or to the corporation with adjustments at the shareholder level. I am not sure how these proposals are to be reconciled with the proposed taxation of appreciation (which would swallow up any corporate income or loss). Passing this question, Dean Galvin would evidently require the continued computation of corporate and business income—but he does not say whether this type of income, like personal income, includes appreciation and depreciation in business assets, such as patents, goodwill, and real estate, or whether such "artificial" tax rules as the immediate write-off of research and development expenses and accelerated depreciation are to be abandoned in favor of the Haig-Simons principle.

My point, let me make it clear, is not to take exception to Dean Galvin's proposals (though I have reservations about some of them), but to suggest that a broadening of the tax base can create, as well as dissipate, complexities; and that it will invite the enactment of "relief" provisions to soften the impact of some of its changes and to restore some of its casualties.

As to proportionality in the tax rate, whether divorced from or accompanying the base-broadening proposal, here too I think that the resulting simplicity has been overestimated. Problems of timing will surely remain with us as long as the tax rate is high enough to count. Parenthetically, I would say that Dean Galvin's estimate of a 13 percent rate would have to be revised upward if personal exemptions are allowed or if, though denied, their absence is redressed by an increase in expenditures. The same would be true of the inclusion of social security and other transfer payments in the expanded tax base. A rate of 20 percent or even 25 percent seems more realistic to me than 13 percent. Whatever the exact rate, it will surely be high enough so that it will make a big difference whether I am taxed on unrealized appreciation currently, or only when I sell the asset or pass it on at death. If a personal exemption is allowed, as Dean Galvin suggests, the problem of income-splitting will continue to plague us, especially with respect to minor children and the undistributed income of discretionary trusts. Depending on how corporate and business income is to be reflected on the individual income taxpayer's return, the distinction between taxable distributions of income and tax-free distributions of capital may continue to be important. Moreover, there are many problems in computing corporate income despite the essentially flat corporate rate that has prevailed for many years, suggesting that progression is not the sole source of complexities in federal income taxation.

## II

Let us assume, however, that despite my reservations, Dean Galvin's flat-rate-broad-base income tax would be a major breakthrough in the war on complexity. Here I interpose a demurrer: What of it?

If simplicity is our major or sole aim, it could best be achieved by dividing up the tax burden equally among all citizens, letting them pay an equal amount per capita. The only reason for using an income tax, which under the best of circumstances is bound to be a complex tax, is that we have somehow arrived at the conclusion that income is a better index of ability to pay than the mere fact that the taxpayer exists, and that it is also better than basing the tax on the taxpayer's age, the number of acres or cattle he owns, his purchases of luxuries or necessities, or his social security number. As I argued in my presentation last week, anyone who favors reliance on income taxation as a major source of public revenue must have at bottom a conviction about its fairness; and if he is pressed for his reasons, I do not know what he could say other than that the income tax performs better than other taxes when judged by such criteria as "ability to pay," "minimum (or proportionate) sacrifice," "reduction of economic inequality," etc. (It is sometimes argued that a proportional income tax has the economic virtue of leaving the determinations of the market relatively unchanged; however valid this point may be when a proportional *income* tax is compared with a progressive one, it carries no weight when we are asked to choose between an income tax and a per capita tax; as between *these,* the per capita tax does least violence to the market's assessment of the value of goods and services.) Having accepted these criteria in making the basic decision to tax income rather than some other taxable base, I see no reason, on turning to the rate structure, to assert that proportionality is *ipso facto* correct because any other principle would require us to make impossible judgments about the respective abilities to pay or sacrifices of persons at different income levels, or about the acceptable degree of economic inequality. Moreover, it seems to me that Dean Galvin himself has unmistakably, though implicitly, accepted these standards, despite the obviously discretionary judgments they require in application.

Thus, his acceptance of a personal exemption in computing taxable income is justified in terms of ability to pay. Similarly, in favoring progressive income tax rates to counteract regression in state and local taxes—which he describes as having "an almost vicious regressive effect"—his unstated assumption is that income is a better index of ability to pay than the taxpayer's purchases or real property. After all the state sales tax and the local property tax are levied at a *flat* rate; they are "regressive" only if measured against income. (Conversely, a proportional income tax may turn out to be "progressive" if measured by reference to the taxpayers' purchases of goods and services.) But *why* does Dean Galvin use income as the base in measuring the regressivity of taxes levied on other bases? Because, I submit, of an unarticulated major premise, *viz.*, that income is a better measure of ability to pay, or of sacrifice, or of economic inequality.

Let me make quite clear that I do not reproach Dean Galvin for employing this premise. To the contrary, I think he is clearly right in doing so; my objection is that he does not make the most of it, by using it in comparing progressive income tax rates with proportional ones. Of course, I do not know where he would have come out if he employed these admittedly discretionary standards as an analytic tool; perhaps he would conclude that proportionality in the rate structure would equalize the sacrifices of contributing taxpayers, or would match their ability to pay, better than progressive rates. My point is that his ultimate value judgment would then be brought to the surface, rather than obscured by a disclaimer of the ability to make such interpersonal judgments.

## III

Finally, I would repeat my argument of last week, *viz.*, that it can be an empty exercise to discuss tax rates without taking government expenditures into account. At several points in his presentation, Dean Galvin linked the tax side of the national budget with expenditure policy, but I think that this link should have been pursued further. Thus, he indicated support for subsidies, rather than tax provisions, to stimulate investment in particular activities or industries, and he also pointed out that public assistance might be used instead of personal exemptions as a method of protecting low income taxpayers against an invasion of the minimum subsistence level.

The interchangeability of tax provisions and subsidies has been much discussed in recent months, and we now have the Treasury's "Tax Expenditure Budget" as an effort to put flesh on the skeleton. While I have reservations about the claim that such an assemblage of estimates can be complete or comprehensive in an objective sense, its underlying premise that tax provisions can be substituted for expenditures is a useful tool of analysis. Its value, moreover, is not diminished by the fact that interchangeability is a two-way street, i.e., that to exclude someone from an expenditure program can be viewed as a method of taxing him. Just as an exemption of soldiers from income tax could be regarded as equivalent to paying them a subsidy, so the exclusion of civilians from the G. I. Bill of Rights can be regarded as equivalent to taxing them. Similarly, for the Treasury's "Tax Expenditure Budget," one could provide its twin, *viz.*, an "Expenditure Tax Budget."

Once this link between taxes and expenditures is recognized, I do not think it is satisfactory to discuss the rate structure without reference to expenditure policy. Thus, Dean Galvin offered, as an example of unfairness in the existing tax structure, the fact that a single man with a salary of $25,000 pays almost twice the income tax paid by a married couple with two children, a salary of $20,000, and $5,000 of net long-term capital gain. If this is unfair, however, would equity be achieved by reforming the income tax in accordance with Dean Galvin's proposal, so that they both paid the same income tax, if the married couple were then to be granted a subsidy consisting of a marriage bounty, a child care allowance, and an investment credit equal to the former gap between their tax bills? Similarly, it seems clear to me that simplification should also be viewed in a global perspective: If a broad base eliminates complexities from the tax law and reduces the time spent by lawyers, accountants, and their clients on what is sometimes described as "sterile" tax-planning, but we then replace the tax concessions with subsidies, I am afraid that the liberated clients will soon be closeted with their lawyers and accountants for another round of planning, and I see no reason to think that the Commerce Department's regulations for the expenditure of public funds will be less complex than the Internal Revenue Service's rules for granting so-called "tax expenditures."

I do not suggest that subsidies and tax concessions are functional equivalents in all respects; there may well be good reasons for using one device rather than the other to accomplish a particular purpose. But the link is sufficiently strong to strengthen the case (which is independently strong) for taking account of expenditures when judging the fairness of the tax structure. As I argued last week, this widened angle of vision does not make the process of judgment any easier; to the contrary, by adding to the variables in the mix, it may weaken the foundations of one's faith. Even so, I think we ought to make the effort to base our judgment on all of the variables, however elusive they may be.

## CHARLES O. GALVIN

I have reviewed the proceedings of both previous Thursday evenings, and as a result of this exercise several propositions come to mind. Let me express them briefly.

This is a rational debate. Let us, therefore, keep the discussion open, preserve as many viable options as we can, or as the vernacular goes, let us hang loose. Let us not confuse rationality with what is popular, politically palatable, pragmatic, expedient, or exigent; these words are not synonyms for the word "rational." There are all kinds of instances in our earlier and recent national history in which views were totally unacceptable to the great mass of the people but had an underlying rationality which, in time, through the process of ratiocination (a good word, incidentally, for this occasion) became the will of the majority. One could cite the changing attitudes on race or on our involvement in Southeast Asia as but two issues on which the national will has changed radically and rapidly. New positions do evolve through the process of rational debate and open dialogue, and not by trading snarl for snarl which often accompanies these highly emotionally charged issues.

Now, as to my position paper, the first part of my case in chief was to carry you to the outermost limits of the Haig-Simons definition for base-broadening purposes. This went very far, very fast, and the immediate and expectable response was some digging in of heels, for, quite naturally, each person begins to think of problems of transition. But this is an important point; we think and analyze the problems of transition, because we are not satisfied with what we have. We think of moving to a new base, not of preserving the base we now have. Thus, I daresay most, if not all, who pass critical judgment on the present system favor substantial base broadening. Examine the Treasury's current tax reform studies and proposals and in item after item there are reflected serious efforts at base broadening.[1] Furthermore, there is a remarkable consensus among the writers in the field concerning the general areas of major base broadening; there will be, of course, the expected quibbling over details and mechanics.

Therefore, there is no disagreement in principle about the desirability of closing the gap between real income and reportable income. The difficulties relate not to principle but to a function of time, a procedural, not a substantive problem. If we accept base broadening as a principle, and I believe we do, then let's set as a goal the time for its accomplishment. For example, the Congress might set each year an approximate percentage of the gap to be closed between real income and reportable income. To be sure, one may contemplate wearily on the number of Congresses, the number of Ways and Means Committee and Finance Committee hearings, the number of Treasury study drafts yet unwritten which will have to pass our way before the goal is accomplished, but given a fundamental soundness for base broadening, and given a national goal to accomplish it, we need only to concern ourselves with the function of time within which we have the opportunity to inform the people of the facts and to secure support for the necessary legislation.

The second part of my case-in-chief was to carry you to the farthermost limits of de-graduation of the progressive rate schedule—a de-graduation to a straight line when plotted against the function of different levels of income. How fares the consensus on this issue? I venture to say that in 1964 no one here present and no critical federal tax watcher raised a whisper of an objection when the upward sweep of the progressive curve from 20 to 91 percent was flattened downward to 14 to 70 percent, a drop of 21 percentage points at the top. I would further wager that if a proposal were made that the top rate of 70 percent be dropped to 50 percent, as the Canadians have proposed for their own system, or 40 percent as the American Bar Committee on Substantive Tax Reform suggested for purposes of trial runs, few critical federal tax watchers would raise a serious objection.

In short, if we are willing to move towards a flattening out of the curve approaching a horizontal line, and

I say we are, then we are agreed in principle on the merits of proportionality and only a function of time, a procedural matter, is the issue for discussion.

If we set as the target date for complete proportionality the same target date we set for complete base broadening, then step by step, and session by session, we can move practically and reasonably towards these companion goals.

Nor do I think that the negative income tax to which I alluded in my position paper, is in any sense a violation of the principle of proportionality. There are various versions of the negative income tax, of course. However, my ideal conception is a low, flat rate of tax on *all* income, with the provision that those below an established subsistence level would have an appropriation made to them through the mechanism of the tax credit to close some part of the gap between their respective real incomes, less their respective taxes, and the subsistence level. Keep in mind that I asserted here the first evening that our economic machine can beat poverty and substandard living. That, too, is a legitimate national goal wholly consistent with the other goals which I have described, and a national goal with respect to which a negative income tax offers a device for achievement. Once that goal is substantially achieved, the need for a more or less general negative income tax falls out. The negative income tax, therefore, need not be permanent; it is transitional in character.

Now, as to Professor Bittker's propositions. Professor

Bittker has stated that the burden of proof is not on the progressivists to sustain the validity of the present system. I say it is. We have had progression for 56 years, sharp progression for about 35 years, and I say we have fouled out and it is time to blow the whistle. If anyone doubts this fact, read the well-reasoned, irrefragable arguments in the three-part Treasury study which was released within this past month relating to the case for tax reform. This is not mere rhetoric. With charts, graphs, statistical data, and other demonstrative evidence the Treasury staff makes out a thoroughgoing, well-supported case.[2]

Professor Bittker says that income splitting questions would bedevil us if we allowed any form of exemption deduction, and income timing questions would continue to be serious substantive issues in cases in which income might be postponed for long periods of time. But this is arguing in a purely abstract way; what Professor Bittker omits here are the motivations that impel people to action. If rates graduate from 20 to 91 percent or 14 to 70 percent, taxpayers, with the help of their advisers, are going to be impelled to devise all kinds of intricate private arrangements and to lobby for all kinds of complex legislation; but if the rate is flat, these impelling factors are diminished to an irreducible minimum. Of course, there would be some splitting or timing problems, but nothing like the volume that we now have.

Professor Bittker's reference to the head, or per capita,

tax in juxtaposition to the income tax is irrelevant. A poll tax bears no relation to income, or accretions to wealth. An income tax is based on net accretions to wealth, and to use the head tax to shore up the case for the ability-to-pay argument is leaning on a weak reed. Considering ability to pay on its own merits, I say that there is no evidence of some substantially greater good to a society because some pay more in taxes out of a given dollar than others do.

In the middle of his paper Professor Bittker makes what appears to me to be a reversal of position which devastates much of his other argument. He discusses the balancing of federal income tax progressivity against state and local tax regressivity. From this two-wrongs-make-a-right principle, he says that the federal tax is not nearly as progressive as it appears to be because Treasury studies show that the effective rate of tax on some taxpayers' real income is quite low. He then makes the astounding statement that, "I wish here only to stress the fact that progression in the federal personal income tax is entirely consonant with the achievement of a national tax burden that is proportional to income. Indeed, given this goal, a significant degree of progression is probably indispensable. To be sure, the broader the income tax base, the less progressive a rate structure will be necessary to achieve proportionality; but if we take account of political realities, including the fact that even the minimum tax proposed by the outgoing Treasury staff was based on a less-than-comprehensive base and proposed a modest rate structure, the advocates of overall proportionality ought to support progressive income tax rates for some years to come." If proportionality is a legitimate national goal, as I think it is, and as Professor Bittker says it is, then to achieve it in such a rough-and-ready, clumsy way is indefensible in our society in this last third of the twentieth century. Moreover, if he really acknowledges proportionality as a system, then the other parts of his position paper seem starkly contradictory.

Even if we were achieving some sort of rough-and-ready overall proportionality in the aggregate, the Treasury studies to which he refers demonstrate beyond peradventure that in the upper income groups there are serious disparities in the rates paid by taxpayers on real income. Thus, Professor Bittker's rough-and-ready proportionality may apply to the mass; it does not apply to individual taxpayers. Under my two-part proposal of a broad base and a low, flat rate, proportionality would be consistently and systematically applied to each and every taxpayer. Moreover, in regard to the proposition concerning the balancing of regressivity in the state and local systems, I think we are overlooking what is occurring in the states with respect to this problem. The most populous states have already adopted state income tax systems, integrated in many instances with the federal system. These are in fact becoming the chief sources of revenue. Thus, the federal and state and local systems are tending to come parallel with one another with the largest amount of revenue in each case being raised by the income tax and lesser amounts by excises, use taxes, and duties, and, in the case of the state and local systems, by the ad valorem real and personal property taxes. This contention, therefore, of offsetting one inequity with another becomes weaker as the state systems abandon their regressivity.

Another one of Professor Bittker's rough-and-ready equity arguments is that investment, or property, income becomes a greater percentage of total income as income rises, and property income, being less perishable than service income, can stand a greater bite. He then suggests that unless we use the schedular system of income taxation under which different kinds of incomes are taxed at different rates, the progressive system accomplishes about the same result as a schedular system; that is, income at the top, being property income, bears a larger bite. This just isn't the case, however. Ask Lew Alcindor if his income at the top in pro basketball is going to be service income or property income. Generalizations like this about the source of income in a complex society such as ours will not bear close scrutiny. Moreover, who is to say that the property income is piled on top of the service income? Might one argue that property income—rents, royalties, interest, dividends—constitutes the base which is sure and steady and to which the taxpayer looks first? He then decides how much service income he can afford to pile on top. Here, of course, we get into the murky area of incentive and its deterrents, about which, admittedly, the evidence is inconclusive. Nevertheless, as I stated on the first evening, we all know in our own experience of highly talented service performers who must deflect some of their energies from performing the skills for which they are best suited to the planning of arrangements to shelter their service income. What tax lawyer has not had to spend considerable time in counseling with a group of physicians regarding arrangements to shelter their professional income? This same time is taken away from the performance of the highly skilled functions for which the physician is best suited. We don't have economic statistics on the quantum of this kind of sidetracked effort, but an educated guess tells me that in the economy as a whole, it constitutes a horrendous slippage in the optimum allocation of intellectual resources.

Professor Bittker then changes course somewhat in regard to his assumption that property income is piled on top of service income and can stand a heavier bite. He states that even if the recipient of substantial income receives all of it in service income, he has more security and safeguards and, therefore, is not really hurt so bad. This is just begging the ability-to-pay question by using a hypothetical case as typical of the mass. It does not by any means follow that earners with high incomes all have greater security than earners with low incomes and, thus, all can stand a greater tax bite with the same degree of equanimity and magnanimity.

Professor Bittker then argues the benefit theory:

"Old-fashioned or not, the idea that governmental expenditures on international affairs, national defense, and public order are of special importance to those who are moderately and well off is very appealing to me. Indeed, I would assert that the benefits of these expenditures increase progressively with income and wealth, and that families below a minimum standard of income ought to be omitted from the allocation formula."

If indeed these benefits are measurable, we pay such a high price in other diseconomies effected by the tax system on rich and poor alike that I find this contention far from persuasive. Moreover, it is wholly contradictory and inconsistent with Professor Bittker's earlier point that overall there is more or less proportionality as to all taxpayers. Professor Gillespie's studies indicate that those with low income receive a net benefit in public expenditures and those with higher incomes have a net deficit in public expenditures.[3] The limitations with respect to Professor Gillespie's studies, however, are such that, as Professor Bittker points out, there are various alternatives for attributing benefits, each one of which will produce quite different results of allocation.

Put benefits aside, however, and consider only the redistributive effects of the tax system as a form of common good. I contend that redistribution can be done far more efficiently and far less indiscriminately and prejudicially than is done under the present system. I would rather redistribute on the expenditure side where purpose and object of expenditures can be rationally defended. Let the tax system remain neutral, but let the allocation of resources be a conscious exercise of public choice on the expenditure side where all can see the ground rules for the expenditures and can review and accept or reject them.

This is a particularly significant point. When reallocation of resources for some social or economic purpose is made part of the tax system, through preferential treatment of income, special deductions, and the like, disputes with respect to these matters, as tax lawyers know, turn on questions of semantics in the interpretation of the Internal Revenue Code, regulations and rulings, and pronouncements of courts. The questions at issue involve the technical discipline of the law as it relates to a particular transactional event.

On the other hand, when reallocation of resources for some social or economic purpose is made part of an expenditure program, as for example, the War on Poverty program with which I have personal familiarity, the parameters against which the expenditure is measured are directly relevant to the social or economic objective sought to be achieved. The expenditure is approved, made, and subsequently reviewed and evaluated on the basis of the social purpose of the enabling legislation.

I would far rather subject the expenditure for a Head Start program, for example, to the scrutiny and evaluation that accompany an authorized budget for this purpose than to bury somewhere in the tax system an educational expense deduction or credit for people below certain levels of income.

Finally, Professor Bittker eliminates from his argument for progressivity the consideration of two important elements: incidence and base. With respect to the first, in the case of goods and services for which the demand is relatively inelastic, the supplier is able to pass along the income tax to consumers in price, or in some instances, he can shift the burden to employees. Therefore, even in the case of taxpayers who for statistical purposes are identified as having paid high effective rates, it is entirely possible that these same taxpayers have shifted the incidence of the tax to others.

With respect to the second matter—base—nowhere in Professor Bittker's paper do I see any concern for base. He says he is for substantial progression. Yet on what base? On some hypothesized new base undescribed and undefined?

It seems to me that questions of base must be discussed alongside questions of rate structure. I said at the outset that these issues are not necessarily interdependent, but there is a practical accommodation between the two issues that must be taken into account in rational discussion.

Whatever our resolution on these vastly important questions, let us keep the discussion open and moving, and for this singularly constructive effort I wish to congratulate the American Enterprise Institute.

# DISCUSSION

# FIRST SESSION

GERARD M. BRANNON, Treasury Department: I want to suggest that we have had our debate already. (Laughter). It was Galvin versus Galvin instead of Galvin versus Bittker.

I take it the substance of your critique of progressivity in the first theoretical discussion was that one could not find objective standards to measure this and it was a matter of judgment, and whose judgment?

DEAN GALVIN: That's right.

MR. BRANNON: Then Galvin arose for the negative and expressed his judgments that a negative income tax was good and an exempt level was good and some mild progressivity, which he called degressivity, was good above that. So that we are in the area of judgment. The questions then are whether your judgments are better than someone else's judgments.

When you talked about excess accumulation of wealth, you indicated a judgment that if it was as bad as the 1890s, you maybe would want to do something about it. But in your judgment 1960 wasn't bad, this didn't require any remedy. So again we are haggling about the degree of progressivity.

I think your theoretical argument falls down and we just haven't really focused on what evidence is appropriate to settle the degree question.

DEAN GALVIN: Let me take the latter part of your comments first, whether this is a time like the 1890s or this is a time like the 1930s.

Yes, I am aware of Michael Harrington's book *The Other America* and I am aware that there are disparities in wealth and income in this society. But, on balance, I am still willing to opt for the flat rate or nearly flat rate and a broadened base. That is going to produce the optimum employment of our skills and resources for the rest of this century.

With respect to the earlier point, I knew I would get the kind of comment that you have made, that "you have yielded away a part of your position." I said that I was being politically realistic, pragmatic about it and was willing to accept either the negative income tax or, alternatively, the basic exemption which creates a degressive effect in those very lowest brackets; I was willing to have some gentle graduation. You immediately ask "What criteria would you apply to effect that gentle graduation?"

This issue does not in any way militate against the main thrust of my principal theme. I am starting with something like a natural-law principle, a basic principle that we ought to go for the flat rate but add that we ought to make, perhaps, some modification in these very lowest brackets for the reasons which we all know about. We ought to provide the basic exemption or the negative income tax, which is a form of the same thing, or a gentle graduation to counterbalance the effect of the state and local systems.

My principal theme concerns what progressivity has done to us in creating complexity and in effecting a drag on the economy. This still applies. The kinds of remedies I am proposing here pragmatically don't upset my goal of a flat rate and broadened base. This is my principal thesis.

MORTIMER M. CAPLIN, Caplin & Drysdale: We have been talking about a taxpayer's revolt and the shock of the nation at finding out that there are 155 people with incomes over $200,000 not paying any taxes and 21 over a million dollars not paying taxes. All of these statistics and most of your references relate to adjusted gross income?

DEAN GALVIN: Yes.

MR. CAPLIN: Have you gone beyond the tip of the iceberg, beyond adjusted gross income, to see how much real income, as you refer to it, is escaping tax? What would the statistics be like if you used that as a base?

DEAN GALVIN: That's a very good point. In the tax studies that we did under the sponsorship of the American Bar Foundation we worked with the tax tapes and the Fed tapes. With the people, time, and funds we had, we decided to program a number of base-broadening conceptions and see what happened.

One of these had to do with the disallowance of the so-called personal deductions and the exemption deduction. What kind of add-on to the base would you get?

Generally we think of adjusted gross as the net business income. We think of the difference between adjusted gross and taxable as that difference which is made up by so-called personal deductions.

In any more detailed analysis of the tax tapes these are the kinds of statistics that should be developed, that is working to real income from taxable income, because that is the base upon which the tax liability is calculated.

The commissioner's statistics are developed, of course, on adjusted gross income brackets. We were working with the data available and not new data that we could develop. We had to work with tapes that we had. But in any kind of ongoing research in the direction that I would like to see us go, the sort of research that Mort (Caplin) talks about is most certainly necessary.

Between adjusted gross income and taxable income your concern is about those items that pull these people from substantial adjusted gross incomes into a no-tax-liability situation?

MR. CAPLIN: I am thinking of the no-tax liability before you reach adjusted gross.

DEAN GALVIN: I don't have raw data from which

to speak in connection with that question. These are the kinds of data that we should develop from the tax tapes as we pursue our research project.

MR. CAPLIN: And pursuing this line under your system, what would you do with such items as depreciation and intangible drilling costs (as in mineral exploration)?

DEAN GALVIN: In a broad-based system if you are going to allow deductions for the use of capital, we have talked alternatively about a depreciation system of rapid write-off, or regular write-off, or just cash-flow write-off, which is the intangible system.

There are some rough statistics to indicate that if we used cash write-off, as equipment is purchased, that is, you could just write it off on a cash flow basis, we would in time come out not too far from the base we presently work with.

There is a terrific problem in transition, granted. But over the long range we would be working with a taxable business income base not too different from the one we presently have.

These are rough estimates, of the hunch type. This is the kind of thing we need to look at.

However, if we had people report on the basis of increase in purchasing power in accordance with the Haig-Simons definition, then we would have to get valuations of properties. If an asset is written off under a cash flow depreciation policy, and then it is valued up on an inventory basis at the end of the year, that item is brought back into the taxable base, because it is part of the purchasing power of that individual. You see the problem that you have there.

If a piece of equipment costs 100x dollars and is worth 100x dollars at the end of the year, then under the Haig-Simons definition there is no depreciation in purchasing power and no diminution of income. If it goes up to 105x dollars in value, purchasing power is increased by five. And that would be reflected in income just as if you had received that 105 for services.

GEORGE J. LEIBOWITZ, Library of Congress: In the tax reform hearings now under way, one of the first subjects concerned Treasury Department recommendations to reduce the incentive value of charitable giving by imposing the 3 percent floor. This gave rise to a lot of comment from charitable organizations that this would damage philanthropy.

What would be the position of philanthropy under your proposal?

DEAN GALVIN: If you have a broad-based low-rate system, then the difference between making the contribution with an allowable deduction and a non-allowable deduction is not as great as it is under a sharply progressive system. The inducement to philanthropy many times is on the basis of the money one saves in tax dollars by making a gift. If that money is not so large, it becomes of minimal consideration. To deduct or not to deduct makes just a 10, 12, 13 percent differential, not a 50, 60, or 70 percent differential. So I think other factors would come into play in determining whether people would make contributions to charity.

If we are thinking of a really broad-based system and a low rate of tax, then many of the inducements that are tied in with our present tax system we have to reconceive. Look at the entertainment industry that depends upon the write-off of the businessman's entertainment tab at high brackets. It is easy to take the customer out because you are charging it off at higher brackets than would be the case if you had a very low flat rate of tax. What happens to all of the posh nightclubs and entertainment spots? You could argue that they would be hurt by low rates, because high rates might actually be conducive to more business for them.

These are adjustments which would take place in the economy. But I am trying to argue for a neutral system that doesn't have the effect of allocating resources one way or the other, leaving it to other economic factors and free exercises of choice as to what a society wants to do with its money.

GABRIEL RUDNEY, Treasury Department: A major justification of proportional taxes is the neutrality feature. You said the proposal would in effect require the switching of needed subsidies to the expenditure side of the federal budget. Can we be certain that we will produce more efficiencies by this method, that is, switching subsidies to the expenditure side rather than having tax subsidies?

PROFESSOR GALVIN: Yes, I think we can.

MR. RUDNEY: You can't be certain.

DEAN GALVIN: How can I be certain of what the future will bring? On some kind of logical analytical basis, however, we can say that a system which indiscriminately induces allocation of resources without regard to the particular kind of activity of the particular business endeavor is not going to do it nearly as efficiently as a more specialized appropriation procedure, where techniques are set up for qualifying for the subsidy, where the expenditure becomes a direct aid to that group of people in the economic activity that the subsidy is especially intended to encourage and to protect, or to induce. I just think that is a better way to do it.

MR. RUDNEY: Speaking specifically to a feature of the law, would this be your position on the investment credit, for instance?

DEAN GALVIN: Yes.

MR. RUDNEY: Or a credit for manpower training?

DEAN GALVIN: Yes. Or education of children in school. This is reallocation of resources for particular social purposes which can be done better through direct appropriation than through a more or less indiscriminate use in the tax system.

WALTER GARVER: I am Walter Garver, independent economic consultant. For a good many years now in this country much of our institutional structure has been hardened around these concessions and special arrangements. This suggests that to get from here to there, to where you talk about going, is somewhat of a revolutionary transition. In fact, it is so revolutionary that I wonder if it isn't self-defeating in the sense that you would have to stir up so many people that nobody would put up with it in the end.

DEAN GALVIN: I was telling Bert Harding (Director, Office of Economic Opportunity) here that I am the chairman of the War on Poverty program in the community from which I come. My friends twit me in this position saying that no organized society in the history of the human community has ever beaten poverty. Nobody has ever whipped poverty and nobody has ever whipped illiteracy, so they ask what am I doing spending time in this program. I think with the intellectual resources and the know-how and the managerial skills that we have in this society today, the technological improvements that we have, we can do it. We have the facilities to do it.

What you say is certainly true. The transition would produce shocks. But if as a community, as a society, we determined that this is the direction in which we ought to go, just as we decide as a society that we ought to try to beat poverty and beat illiteracy, if we say we are going to do it, then the thing to do is to figure out the best way to do it. I am saying this is the best way. And I am recognizing the problems of transition. But once we decide as an ultimate finding of fact that that is the best way to do it, all factors being considered, then we ought to point ourselves in that direction to do it, recognizing that there are going to be these shifts and shocks and adjustments that have to be made but recognizing also that ultimately we will come out with a far more productive, far more affluent society and a better society. These are the goals we set, these are the objectives we try to attain.

I don't think it is self-defeating if a society determines this is what it wants to do. Then the society points in that direction and does it.

DR. JOSEPH A. PECHMAN, The Brookings Institution: I want to go back to the point that Gerry Brannon mentioned. It is not any slight concession that you are making when you reintroduce progression, however small.

DEAN GALVIN: However slight?

DR. PECHMAN: If you want to provide a personal exemption or if you want to offset the regressivity of the state taxes, what you are telling us is that there is something wrong with proportionality.

DEAN GALVIN: No.

DR. PECHMAN: If there is something wrong with proportionality, then we ought to indicate why we are unhappy about proportionality and then argue about the degree of progressivity we want. It seems to me that you simply defeated your own major premise by admitting that you want to reintroduce progressivity.

The other point I want to make is that you don't do what you say, namely reintroduce some progressivity.

I am afraid your 13 percent flat rate would make the federal, state, and local tax system highly regressive, because you would be shifting wholesale an enormous amount of revenue that is now obtained from the higher income brackets onto lower income brackets.

You might offset that by expenditure policies and so forth.

DEAN GALVIN: If you eradicate the tilt against service income in favor of property income, you would avoid some of that too.

But, Dr. Pechman, let me say this. I think that I am really defending proportionality when I make a concession to some general graduation to offset the regressive effect of local systems. I am really shoring up my point that I am for a flat rate. But to get an effective flat rate I have got to recognize the regressive effect of the local system, which you point out. And if I flat-rate the federal system and have a regressive effect in the local system, I have had a net overall regressive effect, and I don't want that.

So I am recognizing an absence of the possibility of harmonization or integration of the local systems into the federal systems. And recognizing that, I am going to have to balance somehow to get proportionality. I am still speaking for proportionality but I am recognizing that it may take a mechanism of progression to get it.

That is a different issue. You have to argue that one out along separate lines from another issue which I raised, which was the negative income tax, or a basic exemption, which Gerry (Brannon) brought up a while ago. Administratively, if we try to tax the first dollar of real income for everybody, we face what I concede are administrative problems and certain serious disadvantages for those for whom any tax on that first dollar would be a substantial burden. Thus I am willing on that issue to go for a negative income tax.

Now, that is a separate issue from balancing to get proportionality with the local system.

DR. PECHMAN: You know, the administrative argument certainly doesn't hold. We tax the first dollar of earning under the social security tax without any trouble. I am not aware that there would be great difficulty expanding the social security tax base to include all earnings, if we wanted to. So surely there is no administrative argument in favor of an exemption. The reason that you are in favor of exemption or a negative-income-tax type of payment is that you believe a poor person does not have ability to pay taxes.

DEAN GALVIN: Let me put it to you in another way. I am willing to concede that in this 1969 society there is a core of poor for whom the ability-to-pay doctrine has definite meaning and with respect to whom we must recognize this ability-to-pay principle. And for that bottom group I am willing to have a minimum exemption or a negative income tax. I am willing to say further that in time, with what I think is the potentiality of eradicating poverty and raising these people to subsistence levels, my need for this transitional arrangement will drop away.

So I am making the concession for transition to a society in which the minimum subsistence would not be a problem. We have the resources to provide minimum subsistence to all of our citizenry.

DR. NORMAN TRUE, Planning Research Corporation: It is not often these days I find myself on the same side with Joe Pechman. (Laughter.) Before he thinks that away—(laughter)—I'll say that while I agree with the thrust of what he is saying, for quite different reasons than those that he offers, it seems to me, Charles, as Gerry and others have suggested around this table, you have got yourself boxed into a set of inconsistencies when you are willing to concede the introduction of some progressivity into your proposed flat rate tax.

One of your arguments against using a graduated tax was that we have other devices that are more effective in eliminating poverty. But if you will allow me to translate "eliminating poverty" into transferring income to people at the bottom of the income scale, I think you are going to be very hard put to demonstrate that any one of these other devices that you suggest is any more or less efficient than, say, a negative income tax would be. I think what you ought to do, if you will allow me to argue on your behalf—

DEAN GALVIN: All right. (Laughter.)

DR. TURE:—is to say that indeed there may be a

social drive, an ethos, in our society for using one or another element of public policy for the purpose of redistributing income.

That allows you to beg the question of whether or not any of those devices are effective in accomplishing that result. You could very well add as a brief digression that those who urge a graduated rate structure in the income tax for that purpose bear an enormous burden of proof to demonstrate that it has any effectiveness in that respect. You could very well say that given such an ethos, we have to be able to demonstrate, on the basis of some other criteria, that one set of devices is superior to another.

You might very well accommodate in your proposal—and in fact, instead of accepting it defensively, actually push it as a poverty bargain—the incorporation of a negative feature in order to make the thing socially acceptable.

DEAN GALVIN: Here is how I planned to write the paper. When I got to that and—(laughter)—started to make the concessions, I was thinking of my opponent next week. I was going to try to pull a little of the carpet out from under him. Maybe I have pulled it out from under myself. Obviously, for some of you I have.

I was going to make this kind of a thrust, to stay with a theoretical analytical argument and argue, just as a proposition for the next hundred years, that we think in terms of integrating the state and local systems into the federal system with an overall income tax shared by local and national government. Then I would have avoided this trap. I would have just stayed away from it.

With respect to negative income and flat rate, to get at what Norm (Ture) is talking about, the social desirability of aiding those who in this time under these circumstances do not have this ability to pay, rather than trap myself on my own ability-to-pay argument, I was going to get over on the expenditure side, stay away from the income tax system, urge the continuance of the antipoverty programs which we now have, which are expenditure-side problems. Perhaps if I had the chance to rewrite the paper, with the benefit of this discussion, I would have avoided the thrusts of Brannon and Pechman and stayed consistently, you see, with proportionality for the state and federal systems and the use of appropriation to solve poverty for those who didn't have the ability to pay. Then I would not have gotten myself impaled on the ability-to-pay argument insofar as income tax was concerned and I would have made no concessions.

That perhaps would have been sharpening the issue better for my colleague next week. But it is a speculation and I chose to go the other way.

DR. TURE: Well, Charles, may I hector you for just one more moment?

DEAN GALVIN: Yes, sure.

DR. TURE: Your last position assumes that the expenditure approach, the war on poverty, really is an efficient way to proceed, more efficient than, say, a negative income tax, because you are setting up as the objective here changing the distribution of income. Unless you can demonstrate—not just intuit that that is so, but really demonstrate with some validation that that is so—then I think you really cannot reject a negative income tax on these grounds.

What you could do, however—again, may I help?

DEAN GALVIN: Yes, sure. Please do. (Laughter.)

DR. TURE: What you could do is to say that there are certain other distortions that are introduced by graduation per se, even with a perfectly neutral tax base, a non-exception tax base. There are distortions associated with graduation in the rate structure, so you are willing to pay the price for the elimination of those distortions by going over to the expenditure side of the budget for purposes of income redistribution, again without any assertion as to whether or not you will accomplish that objective.

DEAN GALVIN: I like that. I like it very much. As one who has a personal experience, a deep involvement, in an antipoverty program and has observed the component parts of it, Head Start, Manpower and Upward Bound and Job Corps and on-the-job training and homemaker services and so on in actual operation, I can make a very persuasive argument that the expenditure side is the way to go at this and not the negative income side.

The setting up of programs which make people productive, the Head Start program, which is a step in eradicating illiteracy, or the Manpower Training or the New Careers program that upgrade productivity among people in a community—these are expenditure programs that are catalytic agents for stepping up the productivity and the literacy rate of a community. That's using expenditures and I stay away from controversy that way. I don't even mention the negative income tax. I stay out of that argument.

I stay away from problems of exemption by going ahead and taxing that first dollar, recognizing that on the expenditure side I am going to take care of particular cases with particular programs. This I could argue even better than I can argue negative income tax, because I have more experience with expenditures.

BERTRAND HARDING, Office of Economic Opportunity: I guess I have to put a word in there on that one. I don't think you ought to run away from the negative income tax so fast. (Laughter.) I commend your commending those programs but—(laughter).

DEAN GALVIN: I thought you would.

MR. HARDING: —the truth of the matter is, if you examine the 24, 25-million-person poverty population, you will find that there is somewhere in the neighborhood of maybe 18-20 million of those who are really either not going to be affected by these programs, no matter how well they are developed, or are going to be affected only 15-20 years hence, as in the Head Start case.

DEAN GALVIN: That's right.

MR. HARDING: I don't think that we can put that problem off for that period of time. As far as I'm concerned and as far as our agency is concerned, the negative income tax is the only way or the most appropriate way to get at that redistribution problem.

DEAN GALVIN: Yes, but you're not going to ditch these expenditure programs.

MR. HARDING: No, no. No, not at all.

DEAN GALVIN: In their entirety.

MR. HARDING: No, no, in spite of what some of the more conservative advocates of the negative income tax think, you are not going to ditch those programs. We are talking about the redistribution problem that's necessary now in addition to these rehabilitative and cycle-breaking programs.

DEAN GALVIN: Yes.

MR. HARDING: So I hope you don't rewrite the paper to take out this.

DEAN GALVIN: No, I won't. (Laughter.)

A VOICE: Shall we take a vote now, Charlie? (Laughter.)

ALBERT W. BRISBIN, Internal Revenue Service: I think that if you buy Bert Harding's exception to your modified purist approach you are led down a road immediately. Five years from today housing may become such a crucial national issue that we may want to use all the resources of government for that one big problem. If redistribution on the lower levels is that big a problem today and you will have cured that most of the way, then you are going to be focusing on housing, on whether or not you shouldn't give some little advantage there to accomplish that goal.

What I am saying is that you are going down the old route, the minute you start espousing negative income tax.

DEAN GALVIN: But if we get the housing, we are going to do that by expenditure and not by a tax system.

MR. BRISBIN: Why couldn't you take care of your low-income person by expenditure as well?

DEAN GALVIN: You can. As Bert says, though, the statistics show there are going to be some people left out. They are not brought into the stream. We can enlarge the program of expenditure, this is possible—

MR. BRISBIN: But there have been programs of guaranteed annual income, for example.

DEAN GALVIN: True, and, of course, but for the Vietnam war we would have had more expenditure in antipoverty over the last four years than we now have. We would be looking, perhaps, at a different situation on the expenditure side than we are now looking at.

MR. HARDING: I really think this is a question of pure administrative technique as to whether the transfer of payment occurs through the tax system, through the negative income tax, or whether it occurs by some sort of disbursement of revenue. I think our conclusion is that the most efficient way to do it in view of the good shape you've got the revenue service in—(laughter)—the most efficient way to make the transfer payment is through that device. (Laughter.)

DEAN GALVIN: Then call it an expenditure program.

MR. HARDING: Sure, it will be.

PETER WEIDENBRUCH, Georgetown University: I wanted to go up the line a little bit from the lowest economic group to the $10,000 to $100,000 income levels that you spoke about earlier. It seemed to me that your justification for suggesting a flat rate was threefold:

First, that the application of a flat rate to a broader base would bring in as much revenue as we are now deriving. I have trouble seeing the relevancy of that.

Secondly, that it will prevent the misapplication of the resources of many in the room here to the carrying out of tax avoidance schemes, because with a flat rate it will no longer be as important to do that. It would seem to me that the base broadening that would eliminate the tax avoidance possibilities would largely negate that reason.

Thirdly, what I think is your most important justification and one that I'm troubled by most, is that it's difficult for one to prove that there really is a greater ability to pay in the 100,000th dollar than in the 10,000th dollar.

It would seem to me that you have shifted the burden of proof to the wrong fellow by saying to me that I ought now to prove to you that the $100,000-income person can afford to pay more than the $10,000-income person. First of all, we have done it the other way. We have all grown up with the assumption that the $100,000 income can bear the burden of a higher rate of tax. I am wondering why you didn't devote more time to proving your side of the case.

DEAN GALVIN: You are making an argument for old times' sake, I think, when you say we grow up with something and therefore we ought to accept it because it's a nice, comfy, secure thing that we know. We know our way through the labyrinth and those of us who work in the field with some competence or expertise would hate to see the thing change because then we couldn't find our way as well. I don't think that's a logical argument for preserving anything, just because we've had it.

Now, with respect to the burden of proof, you say I should assume the burden for the flat rate and not cast it against those who opt for or support the progressive rate. Of course, you are asserting something that's in the realm of speculation. We're working with the progressive rate now. I'm trying to correct the flaws of that system. To bulwark the argument I make for proportionality—I am trying to point out the absurdity of the complexities and the abstruseness of the present system as a reason for trying something else which logically, on any kind of objective analysis, without experience, would lead us to simplicity, to neutrality, and would eliminate the tax factor in what otherwise should be free exercise of choice for investor, producer, consumer in an open economy.

Sure, you can say you can't prove it. No, I can't prove it, because I don't have a system to point to. But I can certainly see the flaws in the present system and I can argue from some kind of abstract logic of trying out a different system.

MR. WEIDENBRUCH: But don't the flaws in the present system emanate from the first issue, the fact that the base isn't broad enough?

DEAN GALVIN: Partly.

MR. WEIDENBRUCH: Having once achieved a broader base, haven't we then come to the simplicity? It's not proportionality that produces simplicity, it's the base broadening, isn't it?

DEAN GALVIN: Progressivity also perpetuates complexity. Progressivity places almost incredible pressures on congressmen to pass laws which relieve some people from the full impact of progressive rates. So you are led right back down the same path from which you have come.

PAUL TREUSCH, President-elect, Federal Bar Association: Why is it that you assume that equating is necessarily socially the more desirable course? Why is each effort to neutralize necessarily thrown in one bag? Everything to that effect is regarded as socially undesirable or at least less desirable than treating everyone as being entitled to the same treatment in the social order. To me, this would push the tax law back 100 years. The whole thought that you can't use the tax mechanism for anything except raising this 13 or 14 percent of revenue is just antediluvian.

DEAN GALVIN: No, I think it's 100 years ahead instead of 100 years behind. (Laughter.) If you want to adhere to the notion that we have somehow got to build into this tax system a reallocator of resources and social and economic engineering, to achieve various social purposes which a society deems desirable, then you and I can't argue about it, because I'm arguing for a—

MR. TREUSCH: But Charlie, take some of the steps that you are going to take to broaden the base. Is it necessarily antisocial to prefer the property owner to the property renter? I mean, this preference apparently must have some social benefit in somebody's eyes, or it wouldn't have been adopted and kept.

DEAN GALVIN: I'm saying that the society ahead of us, not the society behind us but the one we are looking at ahead, is going to become a highly technologically-skilled group of specialists. I think that the service producer must not be put at a disadvantage with the property income earner. They've got to be handled alike.

You say is it socially desirable that they should be handled alike? I say, "Yes." Then you may say, "No."

You say, "How do I know it should be?" Here we fall back on common experience. I think that if we are to have the kind of managerial skills and technical skills, professional skills that this community needs for the next 33 years we cannot put this kind of skill at a disadvantage alongside the ownership of property. I think we have to keep these in some kind of parity.

MR. TREUSCH: It seems to me that it's a question of semantics whether you are going to use the tax as the carrot or you are going to use the expenditure as the carrot.

DEAN GALVIN: Expenditure is more efficient.

MR. TREUSCH: It's the objective that you are trying to accomplish in the social order. If you use the tax mechanism to do it, why isn't that equally effective socially to using some more obvious way to an outright subsidy?

DEAN GALVIN: We're arguing here and this is good. I am hearing arguments coming through to me that sound like people saying, "Gee, isn't this present system great?" And I can't believe— (laughter) — that anybody really and truly subscribes to that view.

MR. TREUSCH: I'm not saying that either, Charlie, but I'm saying let's not throw it all overboard, just throwing the baby out with the bath. There might be some things about a variation in a completely broadened base that might be justified socially.

DEAN GALVIN: Yes, sir.

FRANK GRAY, Lybrand, Ross Brothers & Montgomery: I think that it is a rational debate. Therefore, if you are going to bring something to the Congress, it should be something that will be palatable. There are special interest groups that have concern about restricted stock options, investment credits and other things. I think these things will have to be answered. The paper must be rational and if it's not received too well here there's a good chance it wouldn't be by anyone, although everyone here I'm sure would agree that there is a need, an immediate need for reform.

DEAN GALVIN: You say there are people who have vested interests in stock options or restricted and qualified options. Sure there are. In a highly progressive income tax system, you need this kind of inducement built into the system to encourage executive talent to stay with the particular corporate entity and maximize his services and productivity with that particular company.

But then there are other professional groups rendering equally valuable services in our society who do not have the benefit of that.

MR. GRAY: They like the Keough Plan, which is—

DEAN GALVIN: Well, maybe so, but what I'm saying is—

MR. GRAY: Incidentally there is another contributing factor to this and that is, of course, capital. And to attract capital we do provide the capital gain and the dividend exclusion and other things. These things have evolved with some—

DEAN GALVIN: They have evolved because of sharp progressivity in the rates. Surely we don't argue that. These things have evolved because of sharp progressivity in the rates.

An executive in the highest levels of the income bracket has to have stock options as an ameliorative kind of setoff against the effect of high rates on his salary income. He's got to have compensation in some other form.

If you flatten the rate down, if you had flat rates all along, that would never have happened. Now, you know that. It would never have happened. So rationally that's the point for opting for a simpler structure in which these things aren't necessary.

MR. GRAY: Yes, my barber bought a pole because he realized that he could get the investment tax credit. (Laughter.)

DEAN GALVIN: Well, yes, you may have a high bracket barber, but— (laughter).

MR. GRAY: Seriously, he's a very low bracket barber.

DR. G. WARREN NUTTER, Department of Defense: I've been quiet for so many debates I hope I will be forgiven for making a little statement here. You were very careful to separate the two issues of broadening the base and the tax rate structure itself. I think this has created a bit of confusion which came out a moment ago on the question of the tilt, as you put it, against service-type income.

The primary reason that we treat capital gains separately and differently from ordinary income is, I think, fundamentally to put progressivity in the system. If you were to use the Simons definition of income, you would have to provide some kind of averaging, long-range averaging, of income in order to avoid the sudden shifts up and down in capital gains. So I think that your argument that your system will move the tilt away depends on the two things together; that is, both the flat rate and the broadened base. If you were to separate them, you would have to provide for some kind of elaborate income averaging, which might be all right also.

DEAN GALVIN: Yes, you're right. If we don't flatten the rate and if we have a sharp progressivity in the rates with a broadened base, we have to have some kind of fairly general averaging as we do now to avoid this bunching in particular years.

If I'm going to separate those issues, then I've got to argue as a subassumption that, if under the broadened base, we are to have sharp progressivity—which I do not subscribe to, but if we do for other social reasons—then the averaging is very important to avoid the bunching problem.

But if we have the broadened base and the flat rate, then the averaging problem drops out. But I still don't get your point about the capital gains.

DR. NUTTER: I think the point was just made a moment ago. Why should this system work against property income and so on? Why is it necessary to have flat rates in order not to ? I just wanted to clarify this.

DEAN GALVIN: Yes, that's a good point.

JACOB STOCKFISCH, Institute for Defense Analysis: I'd just like to make a distinction the lack of which I think has muddied some of the discussion. I think when you talk about progressivity you are normally referring to progressivity in the statutory rate, yet operationally the system does not behave that way at all. You cited the figure of 30 percent.

DEAN GALVIN: Yes.

MR. STOCKFISCH: I would like to point out that given the flat-rate system you propose, with a broad base, and then if you start plugging in an exemption or a credit, you can make the overall system operate in a way which might even be far more progressive than the present system as an engine for redistributing income and wealth.

For example, take a $400 credit with a 30 percent flat rate. You pay the credit out like a negative income tax. This would probably be more progressive than the present system. I submit that for many purposes that you are speaking about the issue of progressivity or lack of it is really quite redundant. I think Norm (Ture) was suggesting some points along this same line.

So I suggest that we should distinguish the statutory progressivity, which may or may not be intended by Congress. I don't think it really is intended by Congress. It enables demagogues to say something to people: "Yes, we're soaking the rich." But the operative features are not that way at all.

Of course the system you propose would explode this kind of dualism in our thinking. But I do suggest that progressivity in this sense then is not in issue. This system could be proposed and the policymakers, if they bought it, could choose any degree of progressivity they wanted, which is purely a value judgment.

DEAN GALVIN: With respect to one point you make as to progressivity, however, bear in mind that my figures were mean figures. There are people who are soaked. There are people in the highest brackets who are soaked because, for one reason or another, they do not avoid the impact of the statutory rate. There are others who avoid it completely. So you get a mean or an average that pulls the effective rate on the whole group down.

I am saying that within that highest group there are substantial inequities wrought upon that high-bracket group because of the progressive system.

MR. STOCKFISCH: I wouldn't deny that but, by the same token, the way that system operates it has some very gracious regressive elements too. Some people can and do get richer as a result of this present tax system.

DEAN GALVIN: Yes.

MR. STOCKFISCH: And middle-income people and low-income people often don't have a chance to get rich.

DEAN GALVIN: I make the point, as I did, that the broad middle group probably pays a higher percentage of the real income than the people at either end.

MR. STOCKFISCH: Yes.

DEAN GALVIN: I think that's right.

# SECOND SESSION

HARLEY HINRICHS, Associate Professor at the U.S. Naval Academy and lecturer in economics at the University of Maryland Graduate School: As a former student of Harold Groves I sympathize with your ideological background. However, it would seem that there is a great paradox in your position. You seem to be apologizing for the present system, assuming in fact if you had a proportional marginal rate this system would be proportional. It would seem to me that in fact the present system is a combination of a series of average tax rates which are regressive for some, which are proportional for many, which are progressive for others and which after $50,000 income tend to be regressive again for another large group. So that the present melange of progressive floor rates tends to result in a system which in fact may be more regressive and proportional than we as followers of Harold Groves would like to see.

On the other hand, if you had a proportional marginal rate, say maybe 25 percent or 33 percent, providing a fairly high marginal exemption limit, say of $1,000, maybe there would be no taxes on anyone or any family of any size which earns $5,000 or less. Assuming this system of one proportional rate with high exemption levels, then, you have a system which would be in fact progressive, because the average tax rate would increase, approaching a limit of this, say 33 percent, which is now the average limit for most of the wealthy individuals in our country under some broad concept of income.

So I am saying that the paradox in your position is that the present progressive system in fact is not progressive, while a uniform proportional rate with a high exemption level may in fact be more progressive, looking at average tax rates, than this present system which you are defending.

PROFESSOR BITTKER: I'm not entirely sure that I follow. In part, I was offering as a ground for progression one that seems to be widely shared, even by persons who want, in the end, proportionality. I was saying that I thought progression in the income tax structure was needed even to achieve proportionality.

My own preference would be to go beyond that and try to achieve overall progression.

But I don't think I follow your point if you are saying that proportionality in the income tax structure is more likely to do that than progression. I must have missed something.

MR. HINRICHS: Yes, Basically what I am saying

is that the federal tax structure now may in fact be more regressive in certain elements than we think, primarily because it does tax those who have less than $5,000 of income, it does have within it a social security tax which is the most regressive tax in the entire American tax system, and the fact that it does not effectively tax those progressively above $50,000. Therefore in fact a set of progressive marginal tax rates does not produce a system which is in fact progressive. I am saying that if you had the same proportional marginal rate on income above a certain income, say $5,000, someone earning $10,000 maybe would have an average tax rate of only, say, 10 percent.

PROFESSOR BITTKER: Yes. In other words—

MR. HINRICHS: And someone earning $20,000 maybe has an average tax rate of 15 percent. This may be more progressive. You get rid of the regressive elements which are now present.

PROFESSOR BITTKER: In other words your point is that by increasing the personal exemption, even without progression beyond that, you get a degree of progressivity. Is that it? That was one of the grounds that I also offered for progression.

Of course progression is inevitable to some extent if you have any personal exemption. And the higher you fix it, the more there will be beyond that.

MR. HINRICHS: Talking of that, maybe you would like to say just a word about the regressive elements in the federal tax system which you might wish to abolish:

in social security taxation, maybe integration of capital gains taxation with ordinary income taxation.

PROFESSOR BITTKER: Yes.

MR. HINRICHS: Do you wish to do something about the regressivity which is inherent—

PROFESSOR BITTKER: Yes. I would like to—

MR. HINRICHS:—in these types of—

PROFESSOR BITTKER: —see something done about the social security tax. I know this is dear to Joe Pechman's heart also. I would also be happy to see a lot of changes in the federal income tax structure in the direction of making progressivity more effective.

MORTIMER M. CAPLIN, Caplin & Drysdale: One of the difficulties I have with your thesis is really one of definition. You say that you are in favor of a substantial degree of progression. The difficulty is: Just what do you mean by those terms? What base are we talking about? And after having established a base for taxation, how much progression? Are we talking 1 percent of each bracket or are we talking our present system of 14 to 70 percent?

And then again, against what base? Because, even given the existing base and the existing rates of 14 to 70 percent, they are not meaningful; you don't get the progression that people think they are getting.

PROFESSOR BITTKER: Yes. Let me say, Mort, in response to that, that I debated whether to offer a set of rates, and I know it is Hamlet without the main character, in a way, if one doesn't. On the other hand, my course of thinking is something like this: You already have to make so many judgments that cannot be backed up by rigorous logic in deciding what kind of a tax and what kind of rates to have, that you simply compound that difficulty and find it harder and harder to set out convincing principles in support of any particular rate structure.

About all I can do is express a personal preference which I would put this way: I am not shocked by a spread that is as great as zero up to 70 percent. I know some people are. So I would express that point of view.

I would like to see the spread in rates apply to a broader base than we now have, though not to a base as broad as the Haig-Simons definition would involve.

MR. CAPLIN: (Too far distant from open microphone to produce intelligible recording.)

PROFESSOR BITTKER: I don't think anybody can find that rudder or compass. That is to say, to my mind there simply are no absolutes or other sources from which you can get them. The best one can do is to offer a judgment.

If you ask me, Mort, what would I have said about rates ten years ago, or ten years from now, I wouldn't be able to offer a convincing set of arguments for going to a different rate schedule at any particular time. All I can say is that, at this period of time a spread as high as we now have doesn't disturb me.

DR. JOSEPH A. PECHMAN, The Brookings Institution: You seem to be talking primarily about progression with respect to income. Did you mention other possible bases?

Would you care to comment on whether income is the appropriate base for allocating the tax burden? Or how would you modify income or add to it, for taxing purposes?

PROFESSOR BITTKER: Progression has generally been spoken of, as you know, in connection with taxes on income, and, to some extent, on wealth; occasionally it has been speculatively regarded as a possible principle for taxes on expenditures. And, of course, we have progression in the death and gift tax area.

My preference is for using income as a base, partly because that seems to me adequately to reflect wealth, or at least to permit the base to be defined in such a way as to reflect wealth adequately.

Again, for reasons that ultimately are intuitive, it seems to me income is a far better base for a tax than sales, expenditures, savings or almost any other that has been offered. To some extent my argument for progression as a way of taxing unearned income more heavily than earned income, grows out of a feeling that wealth ought to be taken into account as well as income. That seems to me the most practical way to do it. I have never seen any serious effort to construct any other base that would reflect a combination of income and wealth and to apply a progressive rate structure to it. I think it would be very difficult, if not impossible, to do that. Therefore I am content with the income base as a way of reflecting both income and wealth.

MARTIN WORTHY, Hamel, Morgan, Park & Saunders: In connection with the latter point, you seem to assume that unearned income is piled on top of earned income and that therefore unearned income under a progressive system is automatically taxed at a higher rate than earned income, which you seem to justify from a social point of view.

There may be something to be said for that as a moral matter, but on the other hand, is your assumption necessarily sound? Is it not possible that the earned income comes on top of the unearned income and that a progressive rate structure thus stifles the incentive of the man who has unearned income to work and contribute to society? Doesn't the progressive system destroy that incentive for that individual?

PROFESSOR BITTKER: Let me say first, Mr. Worthy, I don't think there is any basis for thinking of one kind of income as being on top of the other. I didn't mean to suggest that.

Unearned income is a larger percentage of total income as one moves up the ladder, although, as I said, with respect to any particular bracket, you have a range of people who may have a little, a medium amount, or a lot of earned income.

Now, on the question of incentives, as I said at the beginning of the talk, I have simply found unconvincing as the basis for major decisions about the tax structure the argument that incentives are killed. This is a matter of ultimate judgment, obviously. There are so many factors in our society that push individuals in their habits of work, aside from money income, that I don't see any significant dampening of incentives, even with rates as high as 70 percent.

I know, of course, of individuals who say, "I don't want to do this because the tax rate on it will be too high." There is no doubt that one encounters some of that. On the other hand, there are also people who work harder on the treadmill in order to keep from slipping back, when taxes are high. I don't know but what one doesn't cancel the other out.

At any rate, I haven't seen evidence among my friends, my clients, or others whom I have observed, of serious impairment of work incentives, even under the present tax rates.

KIRKLEY COULTER, Senate Antitrust Subcommittee: I would like to raise the question whether the issue doesn't depend partly on the role or the magnitude of the government in our system. When the income tax was established in 1913 or 1914, or whenever it was, I think the rates were on the order of 4, 6, 8, 10 percent or something like that—not over 10 or 20 percent of the breadwinners paid them. You might say your whole tax burden was so trivial, it didn't make much difference, anyhow, which bracket you were in.

In this generation we live in now, it seems the characteristic of the economic system is constantly to grow and create a surplus. And the characteristic of the government is to grow even faster and skim off the surplus about as fast as it is created.

It seems to me, then, that if the government is going to occupy such a large role as it has constantly in recent years, you do reach the point where you can almost dispense with the economic system, since the product of the economy is going to be distributed by political formulae under a progressive tax system.

Now, I grant I exaggerate. But isn't this the direction we are moving in?

PROFESSOR BITTKER: Well, of course, in my comments I took the expenditure side of the budget as fixed. I was concerning myself with the question of how one would raise the revenues required by a given set of expenditures. The question of what the expenditure side of the budget ought to look like involves issues that are quite independent of the question of proportionality as against progression. I don't know that I can, at this point, at any rate, contribute very much to that question.

Given the existing level of expenditures, it is obvious that governmental revenues are going to be very high. The question then, is how to raise them.

PAUL TREUSCH, The George Washington University Law School: How do you answer the attack that was made last week on—

PROFESSOR BITTKER: It's in a sealed envelope. I haven't had a chance to read it. (Laughter.)

MR. TREUSCH:—the idea that you mentioned at the beginning that proportionality is not necessarily evil on the score of adding complexity to the tax laws and introducing the tax motivation as a prime mover in business and personal relations? Are you concerned with this at all?

PROFESSOR BITTKER: Yes, but I think that given high rates, many of the complicating features of the tax law are with us willy-nilly, whether we have progression or proportionality. Timing issues, for example, are complicated.

MR. TREUSCH: Galvin says that he can handle a flat rate of 13 percent.

PROFESSOR BITTKER: I haven't read his speech, but if you look down the list of things that would have to be brought into the base, I suspect that they would entail some complications that you would be trading off against the ones you would be mitigating, not eliminating—by going to a lower rate.

Most of the historic cases that the lawyer regards as the classical foundations of most of our complications come from the 1920s and involve relatively modest rates.

Even with a 13 percent tax, questions of timing would be relevant, whether one has a tax-free reorganization or not is immensely important because it determines whether you pay tax now or 20 to 30 years from now or not at all. I would think that even with a 13 percent rate, assuming that is feasible, those problems would continue, not quite as acutely, but the experience of the 1920s, it seems to me, was that even with a fairly moderate tax rate—

MR. TREUSCH: But we didn't have 20,000 cases in the courts.

PROFESSOR BITTKER: No, that's true. But the base broadening that would be required to bring the rate down to 13 percent would almost inevitably involve a lot of new cases; whether the case load would be 20,000 or only 18,000 or up to 22,000, I don't know, but I have a feeling it would be substantial.

MR. TREUSCH: Do you think the tax bar has an investment in privileges? (Laughter.)

PROFESSOR BITTKER: Oh, it has, but I have never believed that protecting that investment is a very important feature of our contemporary scene.

GEORGE J. LEIBOWITZ, Library of Congress: I would like to get some clarification on the scope of your statement. At certain points it seemed you were talking about progressivity in terms of just progressive rates and at other points you included such things as exemptions and broadening of the base and perhaps even the elimination of certain regressive taxes. I wonder if you would clarify what your concept of a progressive system is. Is it just the income tax system and its rates or are you thinking of the whole tax system?

PROFESSOR BITTKER: One can think of it in several ways. First of all, I've talked of progression with reference to income rather than some other measure like wealth or sales or inheritance or whatever it might be.

One can also think of progression either in terms of the tax burden by itself, taking in all taxes, or in terms of the net impact of government taxes and expenditures taken together.

It seems to me that the latter is not only the most inclusive but also the most sensible way to look at the problem. But it is also the most complicated because it involves immensely difficult issues, as I have suggested, of how you allocate governmental expenditures.

Most, however, seem content to deal with the overall tax burden, taking state, local, and federal taxes all together, though some focus only on the income tax by itself. My preference, as I say, is for the broadest way of looking at it. But I would also want to address myself to those who feel that it is so impossible to allocate governmental expenditures that one must look only at the aggregate tax burden and make judgments about that.

Walter Blum and Harry Kalven, for example, say in their book that one can't come to any useful conclusions about the benefits of governmental expenditures and therefore the only thing to do is to disregard them, looking solely at progressivity versus proportionality of the overall tax burden. At times, however, they seem to be talking only about the progessivity of the income tax.

My preference would be for making a judgment about the whole, but I recognize the very great difficulties in doing that.

MR. LEIBOWITZ: Particularly when you have to

project yourself into such things as changing the sales tax and the social security tax and—

PROFESSOR BITTKER: Right.

MR. LEIBOWITZ:—and getting rid of sales taxes and—

PROFESSOR BITTKER: Yes. On that score, it seems to me that political reality requires one to recognize that state and local property and sales taxes are likely to be major features of the landscape for as long as we can see into the future.

I find it hard to imagine their withering away. Consequently, the income tax has to be viewed, I would say, in a framework that includes the continuation of these regressive state and local taxes.

The federal employment tax is perhaps more amenable to change. But I find it hard to imagine the elimination of the rather regressive state and local taxes in the foreseeable future.

MR. LEIBOWITZ: I thought I heard you say, and I'd like to get clarification on this, that the broadening of the base, that is of the federal income tax base, would reduce progressivity. Did I hear you correctly?

PROFESSOR BITTKER: No. No.

HENRY AARON: The Brookings Institution and the University of Maryland: It seemed to me that your case for progression did not carry us any further than Henry Simons' case for progression. Within that arena it seemed to me you were simply saying that the case for progression is one of opposition to esthetically unattractive inequality.

PROFESSOR BITTKER: Yes.

MR. AARON: Don't the points that you made really boil down to a judgement precisely of that and that the appropriate arena is a broad one?

PROFESSOR BITTKER: I think that's right. I think Simons was right and I wish I could offer an ultimately persuasive alternative but, frankly, I don't think I can. Simons did not expand the arena, to use your term, in the way in which I tried to, but in the end we are faced with judgments about fairness that rest upon all the imponderables that go to make us the personalities that we are.

That's why I said at the beginning that, while I like the concept of rational debate, I think there is only a certain point to which rationality takes us. Beyond that, one is reduced to a statement of his preferences about what kind of society he wants.

MR. AARON: May I say that I think it's very important, however, to broaden the arena and that to carry out the discussions purely within the framework of the tax system itself is really a false issue.

PROFESSOR BITTKER: Yes. Of course, I agree completely with that; but I also have to acknowledge that when you broaden the arena and try to allocate government expenditures, you are required to make more judgments of the kind I described.

DR. NORMAN TURE, Planning Research Corporation: Boris, will you do me a favor and retract this last admission, because if you leave it standing, I don't think there is anything for us to talk about. If you retract it, then we can have some fun. (Laughter.)

PROFESSOR BITTKER: Okay.

DR. TURE: Until ten o'clock. (Laughter.) I think you gave us really quite a rich menu. It's like putting the dinner in front of the diner and then, before he has a chance even to lift the fork, whisking it away. So leave it there.

PROFESSOR BITTKER: Oh, I don't want to do that.

DR. TURE: No, leave it there. I don't really know where to start. I would like to make one sort of nit-picking observation in passing and then pick up one or two points. You responded in answer to an earlier question that you were not impressed with the argument that progressive rates kill incentives. But let me say that that has never been the argument. It is not that progressive rates kill incentives. It's that progressive rates—we're talking about the statutory, the marginal rates—affect relative prices. By virtue of the fact that they affect relative prices there is some response on the part of the people who pay the prices. You can assume that the elasticities of behavior with respect to these price changes are zero. That can be a very convenient assumption but that assumption doesn't make that a fact.

PROFESSOR BITTKER: Okay.

DR. TURE: If, indeed, they are not zero, then there are consequences which you may not be able to perceive at all from your consulting experience or your contact with clients and so forth. It isn't that incentives are killed and by virtue of the fact of the progressive rates someone just stops working. You would have to set up some sort of system by which you could measure the amount of work a man doesn't do because he is taxed more heavily on an income.

PROFESSOR BITTKER: I agree. I was using "kill incentives" in too loose a fashion. But I would say that proportionality also affects, does it not, the price structure because it affects the difference between the value of leisure and the value of work.

DR. TURE: Any particular rate that you put in, even if it is in variants of income changes, has the one sharp price effect.

PROFESSOR BITTKER: Yes.

DR. TURE: The point is: Is it necessary or is it desirable socially, while you are trying to accomplish some other objective, to make that price effect change and change with increasing rigor?

PROFESSOR BITTKER: Yes.

DR. TURE: Let me just take up one of your arguments in favor of proportion. That's the benefit theory which you tried to revive. It seems to me that if one follows your line of reasoning on this, you set up progression in the distribution of tax liabilities—the distribution of tax liabilities, not the increments of the tax—

as a function of the composition of government expenditure activity. Suppose that we were drastically to revise the composition of federal, state, and local expenditure activity so as to focus virtually all of those expenditures to the benefit of individuals at the bottom of the income scale. What you tried to do was to extricate yourself from what could be a very bad box for you by saying there are externalities involved in these programs and the externalities are distributed much more heavily with respect to people at the top of the wealth and income scale than they are at the bottom. But you confess that you are only intuiting this. You offered a formula for the distribution of these benefits but no argument to support it.

Suppose that you then change the composition of governmental expenditure activity so heavily in the direction of favoring the very, very poor that you would have to have an enormous flow of external benefits going to the rich in order to say that the distribution of benefits was not very heavily favored for the poor. Then you would have to say that your use of the benefit theory is justification for the tax rate structure and we ought to have the progressive structure. (Laughter.)

PROFESSOR BITTKER: Norm, in speaking of governmental expenditures that are very heavily in favor of the poor, your term "in favor of" involves judgment, does it not? That is to say, unless your view is that the fact that someone receives a payment automatically means he's the beneficiary of it, I don't know what you mean by in favor of. Prisoners receive free room and board. (Laughter.) But that doesn't seem to prevent economists from saying that the cost of prisons inures to the benefit of persons who are not in prison. (Laughter.)

So that I think we are in the same box, aren't we, with respect to that?

DR. TURE: No, because now you can direct your attention to what is a really critical point in this whole discussion of yours and—

PROFESSOR BITTKER: I hope not for the first time. (Laughter.)

DR. TURE: Yes, sort of. Yours and Charlie's as well. That is to say, most of this discussion about the desirability of proportionality or progressivity, the undesirability of regressivity, has been couched in the discussion of the distribution of tax liability. Then the contradiction here, the fallibility of that kind of framework for the discussion emerges very clearly when you talk about the utility of a progressive tax in terms of changing the distribution of income. When you talk about changing the distribution of income, you are not talking about the distribution of tax liabilities, the impact of that. You are talking about incidence. Unless you've got a good, solid incident theory in which all of us can find some consensus, simply observing the fact that the sales tax is distributed in terms of liability in what appears to you to be a progressive way establishes nothing whatever by way of relief or any other tax to offset it so far as income-distribution effects are concerned.

PROFESSOR BITTKER: I'm not entirely sure, Norm, I follow you. But if you are saying that there is a gap in the discussion of the subject if you can't bring into it conclusions about the second-level impact of taxes, I would agree. The trouble is, I've never seen a theory that I could make use of to proceed. Unless you can give me one, I guess you are saying that you can't say anything useful about this subject at all. Isn't that so? (Laughter.)

DR. TURE: No, indeed. No, indeed. I simply say that you cannot make observations about the effect of a particular kind of tax structure on the distribution of income unless you yourself offer an incidence theory to support your observation. In the absence of any incident theory of that sort, then your observation is subject to challenge by anyone who has implicitly or explicitly an incident theory that is different from yours.

For example, there are some economists of good repute who will argue that, contrary to popular impression, the ultimate incidence of a very broadly-based sales tax is not regressive, it is roughly the equivalent of a proportionate income tax. Well, take that as one assertion of an incidence theory.

PROFESSOR BITTKER: Yes. It would make a difference.

WILLIAM HORNE, JR., President, Tax Executives Institute: Boris, if I interpret correctly what you said about the effect of progression on capital formation, it is a disincentive but yet on the income side you say that this disincentive isn't too bad because there are other factors that are going to lead the individual to go ahead anyway and continue with this capital formation. I wonder, have you given any thought on the expenditure side to any modification of the income tax which would give either an incentive to capital formation or a penalty on expenditures?

PROFESSOR BITTKER: My comments about incentives were primarily in the context of earned income rather than investment, but I would have to say there too, unless Norman or someone else can measure what these consequences are, I find it very hard to cope with them.

What I have read, to the extent it is couched in terms that a lawyer can understand, leaves me with the feeling of great inconclusiveness about those consequences though I concede that there must be some.

Your point was: Could I suggest anything that would contribute to capital formation?

MR. HORNE: No, I say have you looked at any offsetting possibilities for modifying the income tax in order to give some incentive to capital formation or contrarily to give a penalty to expenditures?

PROFESSOR BITTKER: Oh, we've got a good many now, to the point where questions are being raised about whether they should continue. We have the investment credit, accelerated depreciation, the write-off of research and expenses, and a good many others. I suppose if one wanted to move down that line further the investment credit could be doubled, accelerated depreciation could be converted into an immediate write-off of the balance of investment expenditure, and so on.

DR. TURE: Joe will give you a reference for a forthcoming Brookings volume that will give you all sorts of theories to choose from.

DR. PECHMAN: From zero to "N." (Laughter.)

GABRIEL RUDNEY, Treasury Department: Professor Bittker, don't tax concessions force us into examining progressivity in terms of expenditures and taxes? Since concessions serve both social and economic objectives, don't these concessions also determine and expand the public role of government on the benefit side and, as tax savings, don't they also determine the degree of progressivity on the tax side? Shouldn't we then dismiss the examination of progressivity solely on the tax side, since concessions in a sense bridge this benefit-tax slip?

You said before that you had to start examining progressivity by accepting expenditures as given and yet on the tax side we have tax concessions that are in effect implicit expenditures. To look at progressivity solely on the tax side, isn't this looking at it narrowly? I realize you said before that you would prefer to look at the thing totally. But isn't the fact that tax concessions do exist and they are in effect implicitly expenditures, doesn't that force us to look at burdens in terms of both the tax and benefit side?

PROFESSOR BITTKER: I think that may be another reason, if I understand your point correctly, for taking what was described earlier as a larger arena for making the judgment. In other words, I guess what you are saying is that in addition to the importance of expenditures in making this ultimate judgment, we ought to recognize that some tax provisions by serving as incentives have the impact of expenditures and that enhances the importance of taking both together. I think that's right, yes.

ROBERT McCAW, *University of Virginia Law Review*: If you accept the position that we ought to have a progressive tax structure and, at the same time, accept the contention that has been made here that the present system is not truly progressive because of the "loopholes" in it and accept, thirdly, that politically it's going to be extremely difficult to close a larger number of those loopholes, doesn't that put you in the position where you should favor a maximum-minimum income tax structure as an immediate, possibly-achievable way of bringing about more progression in the tax structure, or at least more equality than we have now?

PROFESSOR BITTKER: I have mixed feelings about the minimum tax proposal, partly because I see a whole new area of tax planning opening up which will involve avoiding a minimum tax—(laughter)—by shifting items from one year to another or from one taxpayer to another or from one taxpayer to controlled entities like corporations and so on. I regret that thought, not because it will make any investment in tax expertise obsolete but because it will simply add a new layer to existing expertise.

I am also concerned about the possibility that once an idea of that kind gets into the statute it will then be a growing point for a variety of new provisions as to which one will be able to say, "Well, it doesn't matter very much if we take these items out of the regular tax because they will at least be caught up by the minimum tax." It's a little like the capital gain compartment into which things can be thrown, where one might have had to fish or cut bait if it hadn't been available.

On the other hand, if someone puts to me the question: "How would you feel about the minimum tax if you thought you couldn't get anything else at all to deal with these issues?"—under these circumstances, it's hard to say no. But I don't have much enthusiasm for the proposal, as you can see.

GERARD BRANNON, Treasury Department: I would like to go back to your exchange with Henry Aaron and Norm Ture. I thought you should have stuck a little closer—(laughter)—with the two Henrys, Simons and Aaron. That is, basically, I thought you were leading to the point that one's ultimate judgment about the progressivity of the tax system had to be determined in the light of this whole arena, of the things that government does both in taxes and expenditures that affect the distribution of income. You also could have thrown into the arena the whole government operation with regard to property rights. In that context it was regrettable that you tried to revive the benefit theory of taxation. As Norm said, the externality argument was kind of hard to work into here seriously. Even if there are not externalities in these things, we can make an esthetic judgment that there should be more equality in our society.

With regard to these questions of the effect of the tax system on choices of investors and so forth, I think it's proper to say that these are one of the costs that we face in deciding how much redistribution we want to undertake. It can be integrated into this as an esthetic judgment just the same way that one has to make judgments about incidence in doing these things.

We can disagree on a particular change because we disagree on the real effect it has. This is a relatively objective thing that we can research and discuss. As we make some headway in understanding these things ultimately, though, we have to come back to decide just what kind of a society we want.

PROFESSOR BITTKER: Yes, I would agree completely with that. I didn't mean to give up anything vital in my—(laughter)—exchange with Norman. I understood that he and I were discussing not the economic-equality foundation for progression but rather the overall distribution of benefits and tax incidence.

On that score, I think that if one imagined a different

distribution of benefits, then the argument based on the distribution of benefits is weakened. But I agree with you that this doesn't alter the argument based on economic equality.

MR. AARON: With respect to the benefit theory of taxation, I don't want you to give that up.

PROFESSOR BITTKER: No.

MR. AARON: Though Gerry asked that that be done.

PROFESSOR BITTKER: Yes. (Laughter.) I'll do almost anything Gerry asks.

MR. AARON: The recent work in the past decade or so in the theory of public good is probably based on a continuation of the benefit theory of taxation and it is implicit in all of the work. What the benefits are and how they should be assigned remains a wide open question but if one wants to attach any rationality whatsoever to the purchase of public goods one must rely on something like a benefit theory for the distribution of finance of those commodities. So, far from being dead, it is very much alive. It was revived ten or 12 years ago and it's thriving.

DR. PECHMAN: Boris, I feel that I wouldn't earn the price of my admission if I didn't ask this question. (Laughter.) How can you talk about progression without first having a definition of income? (Laughter.)

PROFESSOR BITTKER: I thought I said, Joe, that there are a variety of possible definitions and you've got to make the judgment against some base. But how one can get agreement on the base is another one of those difficult issues on which there is a wide range of opinion. On almost any base that's within the range that one could use, I would adhere to most or all of what I've said.

But I agree with you that, in the end, if one wants to quantify, you've got to specify the base that you're using.

# THIRD SESSION

DR. JOSEPH A. PECHMAN, The Brookings Institution: I would like to focus on the question of progressivity and leave aside for a moment the definition of tax base. Let's assume we can put Professors Galvin and Bittker in a room and they will come up with a compromise broad tax base so that that is behind us. Let's assume that we do what both of them have suggested and get a very generous negative income tax so that we have taken care of the poor and even the near-poor. Let's say we have our break-even point up to the median income level in the United States, which is now about $8,000 for a family of four.

I am still concerned about the point that you made, Professor Galvin, that you can introduce progressivity into the tax system by way of expenditures. Could you tell me how you would differentiate tax liabilities of a person in your system or differentiate between the net disposable income position of a person with an income of, say $20,000 and an income of $100,000 and an income of a million dollars? You inferred that you could do it by way of expenditures, but I can't quite see how you are going to accomplish this except through rate progression in the positive income tax.

DEAN GALVIN: Dr. Pechman, if you have a proportional or flat rate or a nearly flat rate, then we would redistribute on the appropriations side, whether it be for the war on poverty or some particular kind of industrial effort which we think is important for the economy. What would happen in this connection with the kind of studies that Professor W. Irwin Gillespie (The Brookings Institution) has made as to net benefits and net deficit, I don't know. Even with his studies there are different measurements, different ways of allocating the benefits of governmental expenditures.

DR. PECHMAN: Suppose that because of the generous negative income tax rate your flat rate on comprehensive income without exemption turns out to be 20 percent: I'm giving you a generous margin for the very generous negative income tax. Now, a person with $20,000 of income would not be eligible for the negative income tax, by any definition.

DEAN GALVIN: Right.

DR. PECHMAN: His net disposable income after the positive tax of 20 percent would be 80 percent and so would the millionaire's net disposable income be 80 percent. You said that to the extent that you wanted progression or you wanted to reduce the income of the millionaire—of the high-income people more than the lower-income people—that you could accomplish this objective by way of transfers or expenditure programs.

Is that right? In other words, you don't agree that we should have progression in this sense above a certain level and that level is relatively low?

DEAN GALVIN: That's exactly right. Dr. Pechman.

DR. PECHMAN: Would Mr. Bittker care to comment?

PROFESSOR BITTKER: Well, I think I have made it clear that I would favor progression even so. This seems to be one of the places where the income tax shows up very well by comparison with expenditures as a method of differentiating.

Now, of course you could offer—what would you call it?—a middle-income cost-of-living supplement to persons with incomes of twenty to thirty to forty thousand dollars and finance that by raising the rate somewhat. But I don't see any advantage in this area in moving from the tax system to the expenditure system in order to achieve a subsidy. It seems to me the tax system does it very well.

DEAN GALVIN: Dr. Pechman, let me just make a further comment on that. If we are going to tax people with high real incomes on the basis of a flat rate, as I see it in a general way, the revenue is not going to be very far different from the revenue we now get from those people with low effective rates, as the Treasury studies indicate, on reported income. The revenue is now a smaller percentage of their real income in those high brackets than is the percentage of real income in the middle brackets. I don't see any major redistribution because of proportionality, as I am advancing it here, from what we now have. I see a much more honest system, really, from that standpoint, a much more straightforward system.

DR. PECHMAN: I agree that the actual effective-rate progression that we have in the tax law is much, much smaller than these rates would suggest.

DEAN GALVIN: Yes.

DR. PECHMAN: But, you know, except in the very top brackets there is progression of effective rates. It goes up to about 30 percent on some sort of expanded income concept. I say progression from zero to 30 percent is progression and you would eliminate it. And I think that would be a loss to the tax system.

HARLEY HINRICHS, Associate Professor at the U.S. Naval Academy and lecturer in economics at the University of Maryland Graduate School: Let me first respond to Dr. Pechman's assertion that the system we have now is indeed progressive. Recent statistics show that the income group from $3,000 to $5,000 pays roughly the same percent as the income group from $15,000 to $20,000. This is not by taking simple averages but by seeing that two-thirds of the taxpayers in each of these tax categories pay the same effective tax rate. So I am saying that the system we have now is not in fact progressive for most individuals under the system. In fact, it is regressive for the poor; it is roughly proportional for the broad middle class; it is somewhat progressive within the range $20,000 to $100,000; and after $100,000 it tends to be very seriously regressive. It is only the facade of the system that is progressive. And this is before you add in social security taxes which are grossly regressive.

It would seem to me that there may be a compromise way in between. It would seem that you could achieve a progressive system by a proportional flat rate. If you did have some flat rate but did allow, as Adam Smith and John Stuart Mill many years advocated, some exemption or some elimination of the personal subsistence expenditures from the tax base, then in fact you would have average tax rates which would be progressive, even though the marginal rate could well be a flat rate.

This would in fact lead to a progressive system, looking at average tax rates, but then would provide the neutrality and the simplicity of having the same marginal tax rates for income above, say $5,000 for the typical family of four or five individuals.

DEAN GALVIN: This is what we talked about the first evening. It is really degressive.

MR. HINRICHS: Right. Degressive. Which is basically a continental term which is not too well known in the United States.

DEAN GALVIN: Right.

PROFESSOR BITTKER: In my original remarks I commented on that point, though not by reference to the statistics that you cite, as a way that is very widely accepted for achieving a certain amount of progression.

I pointed out also, in the extract that Dean Galvin quoted in his rebuttal, that many people who say they don't favor progression as a general principle will nevertheless favor it as a way of counteracting regressive tendencies in state and local taxes. I offered both of those as widely accepted bases for progression. I did that partly to lay a foundation for my view that with this much progression, you necessarily have a good many of the complexities that it is sometimes suggested, for example by Dean Galvin, could be eliminated through a flat rate. Anyone who favors progression on either of these rather limited bases is, along with that, it seems to me, accepting the problems of complexity that any progression necessarily gives you.

If your question is "Would my view about progression be wholly satisfied by the kind of degressive rate that results from setting exemptions at some figure and applying a flat rate thereafter?" I would say "No, because I don't care very much for the curve." My view would depend somewhat on where the exemption level was, of course, and what the rate was beyond that, because it makes a considerable difference where you fix the exemption and therefore what the flat rate beyond that point is going to be.

I was not resting my support for progression wholly on that foundation. I think it is a foundation for the progression and it has consequences that I indicated, but that was not my preference.

DEAN GALVIN: If we go back to Dr. Pechman's

original hypothesis: a comprehensive base on which we could both agree, a flat rate and a generous negative income tax, there is no need for an exemption, a basic exemption. The negative income tax accomplishes this by partially filling the gap. We're not talking about filling all the gap, but partially the gap, between real income less taxes and the subsistence level. I think that is an alternative to a basic exemption. I think it is more scientific, more precise to have the negative income tax than just some basic exemption.

MR. HINRICHS: The basic difference is that if you give everybody this $5,000 exemption, then you really end up with average progressive rates, even though you have the same marginal tax rate. This would give you a progressive structure up to a certain point.

DEAN GALVIN: Right.

MR. HINRICHS: Professor Bittker, do you see any other instrument outside of the income tax itself which could give you the progressivity which you would seek, such as maybe in addition to the income tax, get rid of the regressivity in the social security taxes and then maybe add a very progressive net wealth tax which would affect in a sense the four million individuals in the United States or the 2 percent of the population who in fact hold one thousand billion dollars worth of assets, one trillion dollars worth of assets. A 1 percent tax on this body of wealth would yield the same amount as the surtax, ten billion dollars.

Do you see any other instruments which would give

you the progressivity besides the income tax? Why seek it all there?

DEAN GALVIN: He did suggest an accessions tax as a substitute for the present transfer tax system.

PROFESSOR BITTKER: I think those ways could accomplish the purpose somewhat, and within certain limits expenditure programs do also. But by and large the basic emphasis ought to be, and I think has to be, on the income tax if you want to achieve any significant amount of progression.

Your suggestion was an annual tax on net wealth like the local real property taxes. This would probably require a constitutional amendment. But it would be a possible way of achieving that result, yes.

HENRY AARON, The Brookings Institution and the University of Maryland: It seems to me, Dean Galvin, that your position is really an argument over form only and not of substance. The reason I suggest this is that it seems to me you could have answered Joe Pechman's position by saying I can get really all the progressivity you want through a system that fits the form you describe.

How? Well, if you want progressivity to run to a million dollars, simply levy a tax which would reduce the millionaire's net disposable income to the point at which you want it left and provide what might be called a negative income tax for everybody else below that point, with benefits graduated negatively with respect to income, expenditure benefits. And then you have all that progressivity.

If you can have any degree of progressivity by marrying the appropriate negative income tax to a proportional income tax, what is the big deal? Why worry about proportionality? (Laughter.)

DEAN GALVIN: You are misreading my basic position. I have no desire to transfer, to redistribute income of high-bracket taxpayers. I'm talking about a proportional rate across the board. I think Dr. Pechman suggested that I would redistribute. The only redistribution I'm talking about is the redistribution that would occur in a negative income tax and the general redistributions that occur because of the budgeted expenditures. The war on povery is a redistribution to which we all contribute. I detected in what Joe said that he thought that I am trying to take people up at the upper brackets and redistribute out of them especially. I'm not.

MR. AARON: I'm simply saying that regardless of what your redistributional goal is—a big redistribution or none—you can accomplish it through appropriate jigglings on the expenditure side within the framework of a proportional tax system.

DEAN GALVIN: We do. Yet, that's right.

MR. AARON: Then why worry about the proportionality or some progressivity on the income tax side if any distributional pattern that one might be interested in can be accomplished within that framework?

DEAN GALVIN: Because we should not have in the tax system social and economic engineering, where it can't be seen. We should expend through appropriation where it can be seen and evaluated and reviewed on its own merits.

In a war on poverty program I would a lot rather have an identifiable appropriation to a head start program than to bury such a program in some type of tax credit of general application for people with incomes below a certain level. It can be argued for either way. You could say "Let's just give everybody with certain incomes a credit for pre-primary school education."

I would rather put this kind of program on the expenditure side where we can evaluate the program for what the expenditure is designed to accomplish and not bury it as a credit. Both of these have a redistributional effect. But I think the use of the expenditure side is the much more rational one, the much more defensible one.

MR. AARON: The appeal of proportionality escapes me if the object is to lay one's cards entirely on the table. If one wanted to adopt a single rule from which one would move to the expenditure side so that all one's cards were open and above board, it seems to me the lump-sum approach is a very appealing one. Then indeed any form of imposing excess burdens or extra burdens on one person in comparison with those imposed on another person would be clearly visible to all.

The case for proportionality, it seems to me, then

gives way to that for an equal tax levied on everyone.

DEAN GALVIN: We are trying to make a tax system that has a neutral effect on consumer investment and business choice.

MR. AARON: But the best one for that is the lump-sum tax, not graduated with respect to income.

DEAN GALVIN: It's a flat rate of tax on income, from whatever source. That's the best way to do it. Then when we have the revenue in the national treasury, we decide how best to spend this to accomplish the various social and political and economic objectives of the particular administration in office, through the legislative process, executive implementation, and so on.

But the tax system itself remains neutral if it is proportional, with a broad base and a low flat rate.

DR. G. WARREN NUTTER, Department of Defense: Since his name has been mentioned, I would like to get down to Henry Simons. I want to speak here as a former student of his. I am not sure how many others there are in the room.

As I recall Henry Simons' approach to the income tax or tax problems in general, he always emphasized that the criteria of the goodness of the tax depend on three kinds of effects: the effects on equity, the effects on inequality, and the effects on efficiency. I am afraid that some of this distinction has been lost in the discussion up to this point. The important fact is that there are different means of attaining each of these objectives and the objectives are not always consistent.

I would like to focus for just a moment on this specific question of progressivity in marginal as opposed to average rates. I haven't heard much mention so far of the effects on efficiency that progressive marginal rates are likely to impose; that is, the inefficient consequences, the effects on incentives, to put it in its crudest terms, and so on.

It seems to me this must be taken into account. If one is interested in progressivity and can achieve it with a minimum impact on the efficiency of the economy, not merely in terms of the wastage of good lawyers' resources and accountants' resources, but also other people's resources in the sense that they will work less if they are going to be taxed progressively higher for each additional unit of effort, this must be taken into account. It seems to me this is an argument, Dean Galvin, that you haven't emphasized as much as you should. This is something that should be thrown into the pot.

The question of broadening the base is important from the point of view of equity, equal treatment of equals. Progressivity in itself is an issue in the whole question of inequality, whether or not we wish to diminish inequality. Then we have to decide to what degree we wish to diminish it. This is the critical issue.

I don't think anybody suggests the tax-expenditure structure should be aimed at increasing inequality. It is bound to have some effect and, of course, this is the difficult question to solve. Suppose we focus on the question of efficiency. If we were to try to devise a system which achieves all three in the best manner, what would it be?

DEAN GALVIN: In my position paper the first evening I specifically made the point that in this last third of the twentieth century I think more and more we are going to be relying on special skills, we are going to be concentrating more on the service provider and we will have to pay more attention to the kind of income that he earns and how it is taxed. The astrophysicist, the mathematician, the heart transplant surgeon, these are the people who are going to be the backbone of our civilization in these years ahead of us.

Therefore I am very keenly conscious of the deterrent to these people, the dampening of incentive with respect to those who are wholly exposed to present progressive rates or whatever progressive structure you have. These are the same people who can't defer income who do not have property investments which give them very much in capital gains, who are not in the position of having corporate reorganizations and sheltered income of one kind or another.

I am very much concerned with them. I am not nearly so concerned about how lawyers and accountants are going to get along because I think there is going to be a lot of business for them from now on. But I am concerned about those technical skills in the society which we need to encourage.

I do think and I do assert and I did assert again tonight that there are inefficiencies in a progressive system in encouraging these kinds of skills. I said tonight and I said the first night that there is a tremendous slippage in intellectual resources as a result of the progressive system which hits the service provider more seriously and more directly and more immediately than it hits the one who has property income.

PROFESSOR BITTKER: I stressed in my presentation last week the first two of Henry Simons' criteria. With respect to efficiency, I contented myself with a disclaimer: I am not an economist. I might have added that it was Mr. Nutter who selected me to present a position here anyway. (Laughter.) And I added my intuition about the effects on incentive of progressive taxation—the lack of a debilitating impact on incentives.

Norman Ture took me to task for relying so heavily on intuition. I should have responded in part that I have to look to the economists, and the best I have been able to get from their work so far does not persuade me that progression's impact on efficiency is very serious. Now, I may be wrong. Though I have heard a good deal from individuals in the way of complaint, I simply haven't observed any really significant alteration of their behavior.

Mr. Ture said that the unseen hand of economics is working there all the time, even if I don't see it. (Laughter.) And that may be. But I have to ask whether you can get a consensus of the economists here,

Mr. Nutter—(laughter)—on the consequences of progression.

DEAN GALVIN: This is Simons writing 31 years ago. (Reading.) He says: "The result"—speaking of the tax system—"is a decorative sort of progression, yielding much discussion, much indignation, and very little revenue and a total revenue system resting largely on taxes borne by persons far below the level of the income tax exemptions. Moreover, the whole procedure involves a subtle kind of moral and political dishonesty. One senses here a grand scheme of deception whereby enormous surtaxes are voted in exchange for promises that they will not be made effective." (Laughter.) "Thus politicians may point with pride to the rates, while quietly reminding their wealthy constituents of the loopholes. If we had a more moderate sort of progression"—and this is Simons speaking—"a scale of rates which responsible leaders really approved, it would be less difficult to obtain the urgently necessary changes in the basis of the levy of this tax base. It is high time for Congress to quit this ludicrous business of dipping deeply into great incomes with a sieve."[1] (Laughter.) So much do things seem to change so much do they remain the same. (Laughter.)

This was written 31 years ago.

DR. NORMAN TURE, Planning Research Corporation: I'd like to pick up just a phrase of your initial response to Dr. Nutter as a vehicle for seeing if I can focus on what seems to be the fundamental confusion, as I perceive it, in this discussion. You said "whatever progressive structure you have," and it is clear that you cannot possibly mean that in the context of any of your discussion up to this point. You really do not care, insofar as I can perceive from what you have given to us, very much at all, if at all, about progression when it is conceived of in the sense of the effective rates of tax.

You are focusing on and criticizing progression only with respect to the marginal rate structure.

I give you these alternatives. Suppose that you could have, by virtue of one form of negative income tax built into a tax system, a very steep progression of effective rates of taxes, tax liability provided by whatever it is you define as income over virtually the entire income range and suppose you could have a perfectly flat marginal rate applied to any incremental dollar of income throughout that range.

In contrast, you could have a very steeply progressive marginal rate structure and, in fact, in terms of the effective rates, virtually no progression at all.

Now, as between those two—

DEAN GALVIN: How did you do this last one, though? How do you accomplish this last point: steeply, marginally progressive, no—

DR. TURE: Very much the way we have it today.

DEAN GALVIN: Very much the way we're doing it now?

DR. TURE: That's right.

DEAN GALVIN: But it's done unevenly, it's done

raggedly. Some people actually do pay progressive rates.

DR. TURE: That's fine. We'll, just for the sake of the argument, just to get the issue clear, assume that the average effective rate for any income interval has a very small standard area around it, a very small dispersion around it, but everybody is, in that class, closely clustered.

DEAN GALVIN: All right. Okay, then.

DR. TURE: But that's just to eliminate the noise in the argument.

I'm interested in what Boris' response is going to be to this, because it seems to me that the full thrust of his argument indicates that he ought to be very happy about eliminating these, if these are the effective choices, about eliminating graduation in the marginal rates. All of the thrust of your argument, Boris, seems to be: Let's get very brisk progression with respect to effective rates of tax, and you don't really care very much, so far as I can see your argument going, about the marginal rates structure. I think there is a very important issue here. If, in fact, you can get an effective tax to conform with your preferences about the distribution of tax liability and get that with a flat rate, you ought to be very much in favor of it. For example, one of your arguments was that you could see no real saving in terms of effort in changing the allocation of income within a family unit, changing in timing of receipts and deductions and so forth. That would come from the kind of thing that Charles is suggesting, that is, a very broad base and a flat rate tax.

Suppose you have the Rolf type of negative income tax. Suppose you have that combined with the very low marginal rate, say 20 percent. There is, under that kind of system, no tax advantage to be obtained from the reallocation of income among family members.

DEAN GALVIN: But there would be for timing. There would be in the long term.

DR. TURE: The timing advantage would have nothing to do with getting yourself into a lower rate bracket. It would have only to do with the imputed interest on holding back the tax payment, a much less powerful incentive than exists today, where there is a discount function associated with this and also, you can plan to get into a lower rate bracket in time.

DR. PECHMAN: May I interpose here?

DEAN GALVIN: Yes.

DR. PECHMAN: I think Norman is quite right. I think we ought to focus, because this is what the purpose of the discussion is on: Is progressivity desirable.

It is true that you can get a goodly degree of progression in your income tax structure if you have a flat rate tax with a Rolf-type credit.

DR. TURE: May I add at this point, incidentally, that there is no cutoff point on the progression.

DR. PECHMAN: One possibility for a Rolf-type credit is that you have a flat 20 percent rate with $1,200 credit per person.

A VOICE: Refundable?

DR. PECHMAN: Yes, refundable. Now, actually, I think my reckoning is correct, that the net tax of a single person at the $20,000 level would then be 16 percent. At the $2 million level it would be very close to 20 percent. It wouldn't be quite 20 percent. This goes to Mr. Nutter's question too.

We now would have eliminated the question of comprehensiveness of the tax base because we now all agree on the definition of comprehensive tax base. Would you be satisified with the difference between 16 and 20 percent effective tax rates between incomes of $20,000 and $2 million?

I say that that's too little.

PROFESSOR BITTKER: I would too, and I have the feeling that Norman was trying to put something across on me. (Laughter.) He described it in such an inviting way that I was suspicious.

DR. TURE: Lest this charge of my being devious stands—(laughter).

DEAN GALVIN: Let me try the Rolf credit. Are you using credit as credit or as deduction?

VOICES: Credit.

DR. TURE: Credit. You actually give the man the money.

DEAN GALVIN: So on $20,000 at 20 percent the tax credit would be $4,000.

DR. PECHMAN: By this a family of two would be $800.

DEAN GALVIN: It would be $800.

DR. PECHMAN: And he said net rate—

DEAN GALVIN: The net rate would be 16 percent.

DR. PECHMAN: Sixteen percent, that's exactly right, for a married couple. And I think you have to focus on that point, Charlie. I think most people would be appalled if you told them that you are satisfied with effective progression of that sort.

(Several people talking at once.)

DR. TURE: Some people really ought to be challenged on their emotional reaction to this since where effective progression ought to count is where people mostly are. If you could have devised through the Rolf type of approach a system which was steeply progressive, much more so than it is today in the income range of zero or a negative income up to, say $20,000 or $25,000 and very, very moderately progressive thereafter, would that not be vastly preferential to a system which is scarcely progressive at all up to $20,000 and zooms up thereafter?

I don't really see what the big deal is about making sure that there is a higher effective rate of tax on the guy who has $150,000 income than there is on the guy who has $100,000 income. I don't really see what the social policy issue is in there. I think people who are really concerned about effective progression, in the sense of what is the distribution of tax liabilities, are concerned with the vast bulk of the taxpaying population who are not in income ranges substantially above $20,000 to $25,000.

DEAN GALVIN: Now look. Dr. Pechman says people would be appalled but you say, and it is the product of the Treasury studies, that there is actually now a regression in effective rates at these upper brackets. Are we then more appalled at that? Would we be less appalled if it were flat?

DR. TURE: Charles, can we ask the question—

DEAN GALVIN: Are we less appalled?

DR. PECHMAN: I'm not saying that the Rolf credit system would not be an improvement over the present system.

DEAN GALVIN: You're not saying that.

DR. PECHMAN: I'm not sure it would be an improvement over the present system. All I'm saying is that if you are talking about progressivity, you oughtn't to throw out the baby with this kind of bath, you see, you take a bath, but you also have a little bit of progression left in the system.

DEAN GALVIN: Well, how much progression do you want? How much progression?

DR. PECHMAN: That's a matter of judgment but apparently your judgment is zero or virtually zero.

DEAN GALVIN: Yes, because I think as soon as you try to make a judgment that is not zero, that the line on the graph is not flat but has to turn up at the end, then you begin to bring in these other motivations that compel legislation to correct the unintended hardships at the upper end of the line. Then you start complicating the legislation, and we're back where we are now. I think it leads you into the morass we now have. The flat rate won't do that because of its neutrality.

JACOB STOCKFISCH, Institute for Defense Analysis: Dr. Pechman will have his chance to respond but I think he would really like to soak the rich, so to speak, in the tradition of the Wisconsin Populists. (Laughter.)

DR. PECHMAN: I just would like progression. (Laughter.)

MR. STOCKFISCH: But I'd like to observe that apparently it is not Congress' intention to do that and Congress pretty well knows what it's doing but it does it in a devious way. (Laughter.)

DEAN GALVIN: What you just said about Dr. Pechman, though, doesn't apply to Dr. Ture, does it? Are you a Populist from Wisconsin?

DR. TURE: No, indeed. (Laughter.)

PROFESSOR BITTKER: On the "soak the rich" proposal, you know the statement that it's wrong to marry for money but that there's nothing wrong with falling in love where money is. I think Joe might have said of progression that he's not trying to soak the rich but, on the other hand, he'd be happy to have progression wherever it begins to take hold. (Laughter.)

MR. STOCKFISCH: One point I think Dean Galvin has overworked a bit. He has said it a number of times that he favored expenditure programs as the way of distributing the goodies, that this was more rational.

I would like to observe that I think there is a tendency often to compare a rational budgetary process with a program—rational program evaluation process, which by and large simply doesn't exist in this town. (Laughter.) Indeed, if you tried to go to the Department of Agriculture or the Bureau of Reclamation and asked them who is really benefiting from some of these projects or programs they either wouldn't know or, if they did know, they certainly wouldn't make it known because it would probably be scandalous if it were made known.

So I might add there is normally a tendency to compare, for example, an operative sales tax or property tax system and much of its messiness with this ideal, good old-fashioned Wisconsin type progressive income tax which again doesn't operate in the true sense of the word. I would suggest that it's strictly an empirical question as to whether using tax subsidies or credits as contrasted with explicit spending programs is the most efficacious in achieving social objectives. Thanks to what the Treasury has recently done, I think the Treasury can be much more explicit about making known who benefits from tax devices because taxpayers do have to make an explicit claim and you can find out by name and address, if necessary, who gets those benefits.

But try and find out, say, who is benefiting from a reclamation project in a particular area. It's a pretty difficult task. I don't want to labor this but I think that we should put this in a proper perspective.

Finally, I have to register a strong view that this notion about sales taxes and property taxes being regressive simply doesn't stand up. It's a rather peculiar partial-equilibrium form of price analysis which enables one to argue that and, therefore, it's not valid. Or you have to have some rather special monetary assumptions to make the so-called forward-shifting argument stick. I could never understand how people could make that assertion and not also argue then or defend the notion that the personal income tax would not be shifted forward as well.

Roughly speaking, I would assert that most sales and excise taxes tend to be equally diffused. They make some consumers worse off, others better off. Property taxes tend to stick on the earnings of property and, to those who have special reservations about taxing unearned income, we've got one in this actual property tax, even though there are some inequalities there. The most regressive tax system we have is one which is again purposely designed to achieve that effect, which is the payroll tax, and most people have been rather silent on that.

PROFESSOR BITTKER: Mr. Stockfisch, in your skeptical remarks about expenditure policy you took the words out of my mouth but that's not going to keep me from adding a few more. (Laughter.) It has become very popular in the last couple of years to contrast what is said to be the burial of concessions in the tax system so that they never come to public light and are never reviewed by Congress, with what seems to me a highly-idealized view of the treatment of expenditure policy by Congress.

I dare say that the public is better informed on an issue like percentage depletion, let us say, than on agricultural price supports or veterans' benefits. Perhaps, in view of your professional background, we could add defense expenditures. It seems to me also a mistake to accept the view, which also is frequently floated, that provisions, once they get into the tax code, go totally unexamined forever but that expenditure programs are reviewed *de novo* every year or two as though they had no momentum of their own.

I don't say there is nothing to the claim that there are differences, but it does seem to me that a highly realistic view of the tax side has been compared to its disfavor, with a romanticized view of the expenditure side of the budget.

DEAN GALVIN: I don't agree with you at all. (Laughter.) I think you're mixing two points here. You're blaming inefficient management over on the expenditure side, or you're advancing the position that because management is inefficient over in these various departments of the government, judging that this then is an argument for continuing this monstrosity that we now have. That doesn't follow and you all know it. It isn't a fact to say that expenditures aren't reviewed.

We do have review of aid programs. The budget is slashed in various departments. There are requests that have to come forward as to what we can economize on. If all of this is not so, then the American people certainly are being deluded by what's being told to them in the press. I don't think it follows that they know more about the concessions that are buried in the tax law and less about defense contracts and how much aid goes to Peru.

It may be that the public doesn't have any information about either but I say that the aid program, or the expenditure program, can be more easily defined, traced, and identified and can more readily be the subject of a congressional hearing than can these concessions be in the tax law. And in the ongoing working of the system, the expenditures are more nearly likely to be reviewed, if they get out of line, than will be the case in the tax system.

DR. TURE: Why don't we compromise, Charlie, and say there's about an equal amount of guff of a doctrinaire nature with respect to expenditure policies. (Laughter.)

GERARD BRANNON, Treasury Department: I would like to relate this recent discussion to the first question that Dr. Pechman asked, namely, what did you intend to do on the expenditure side to make a $20,000-a-year-man somewhat better off relative to his income than the million dollar man?

One answer that you could have given him at that

point was, "Well, we can provide free public schools." Public schools do provide something like a per capita benefit, but they are more beneficial, relatively, for a $20,000-a-year man than a $2 million-a-year man. The same sort of thing is done in providing free public parks and a number of other services, even without getting into questions like defense, where you have to argue on allocation.

It's not clear that it's always better to put progressivity on the expenditure side. It may be that there's a good reason for doing this in the public school area, but on public parks one can ask the question: Wouldn't it be better, if you really want to make the $20,000-a-year man a little better off than the $2 million-a-year man, to give him a big benefit in taxes and let each of them decide whether or not they want to pay an appropriate fee to use public parks?

DEAN GALVIN: Well, Dr. Brannon, of course you raised a whole lot of issues in your comments there. It seems there are two things, Dr. Pechman's first statement about redistributing from the higher-income groups to the lower-income groups by expenditures. I have no particular kind of expenditure in mind, putting the negative income tax aside. The kinds of expenditures that are made for public parks and schools and education and so forth benefit all. It may be that you could identify particular expenditures that benefit the lower-income groups more and to that extent there is a redistribution.

I am not pushing redistribution. I am saying, if the Congress in its infinite wisdom decides that there has to be some public program, that there is some social purpose to be served, it's better to do this on the expenditure side, whatever that program may be decided to be as the popular will, than it is to do it in the tax system.

I have no particular expenditure in mind. You cited a few instances there which are certainly germane to the discussion but I am not trying to advance redistribution on the expenditure side as an objective. If the social purpose is dictated that this or that particular expenditure ought to be made for this or that purpose and if it benefits the lower-income groups more than higher-income groups, then that's redistribution. I'm not advancing it though as an integral part of my argument.

DANIEL J. EDWARDS, Department of the Interior: I'd like to pick up a couple of ideas that Stockfisch and Ture have thrown out that are sort of off the question.

Haven't we unfortunately reached an intelectual quagmire in this discussion? Let me assert, which seems to be the approach here, that if there is anyone from the uncommitted middle who had attended this seminar the odds are you wouldn't have convinced this person to go into either one of your positions. (Laughter.)

If I might speak from the most abstract and make a very heroic assumption: Let us assume that all economists, lawyers, and accountants agreed to some decision here on changing the tax structure and went up to Congress with this proposal. What would happen?

It seems to me we'd be shot down in the Finance Committee and the Ways and Means Committee. The reason is that these committees represent very powerful positions. The quagmire you run into there is that we as a society are really not prepared to admit the real cost of the political process. For example, Herbert Alexander has suggested that the total cost of all political campaigns in 1952 was only $140 million, in 1964 it was roughly $200 million and, if you extrapolate this, I assume that the 1968 campaigns would have been roughly $250 million.

When you put that cost of the political process against, for example, the assertions on the Hill the last three weeks that the redistribution of income from the consumer and the taxpayer to the oil industry alone amounts to between $4 billion and $7 billion a year, this costs us roughly 35 times what the cost of the political process is each year.

Norm Ture's point is that you have not presented evidence for what the reactions would be to a change in the real prices here, which any change in the tax structure would be. I would suggest that maybe what we need here is another rational debate to set out what the real cost of the political process is.

Here is an article which is now a classic in the field of oil depletion which I may quote, since you quoted from Simons: "The protracted debates on this subject which have become *de rigeur* whenever a tax provision is being considered make demonstrably clear that value judgments cannot be finally derived from the interchange of ideas because factual data are incomplete and inconclusive. Choices of action must be made on the basis of considerable accumulation of raw economic statistics not now available. If such information were so compiled that it would not proselyte a particular conviction or support some preconceived objective, the reasonable minds within the industry, the Treasury, and Congress could arrive at sound decisions to set the matter at rest.

"Any contemplated change in policy, therefore, requires thorough study to determine whether imbalances in resources may result; this is an area in which empirical, trail-and-error testing is foolhardy.

"The cost of detailed macroeconomic and microeconomic analyses would, of course, be substantial but probably no greater than the amounts now spent to debate the matter in each new session of Congress." [2]

DEAN GALVIN: That's the most beautiful rhetoric, isn't it? (Laughter.) I agree with every word of it. Tonight we are trying to polarize positions so that the middle group can find its own level. We, to some extent, staged this so we would polarize it. That's the purpose of the debate. Each one of us can advance with less vigor and more vigor some of the positions that we put before you.

But you've touched on a point with respect to the gathering of data that I feel very strongly about. As a result of the study of the Committee on Substantive Tax Reform of the American Bar Association under the American Bar Foundation grant, it did become clear to us that we are all dealing in an area in which the paucity of information is incredible. We don't know what the tax system really does and to prove some particular point with respect to the present system is a proof that has to be made on the flimsiest evidence. To try to work from such evidence and then to extrapolate to what it might be if we changed the system, is of course, inference on inference which gets us into errors compounded. But maybe this is where we begin. Maybe this is where our rational debate should start, some kind of a debate of methodology as to how we might begin to collect the kind of information that we need, to undertake the sort of major study that the Canadians did. They had to gather up information by the pound, by truckloads, to get at the kind of study that they undertook. Even in the Canadian study there is a short-fall in the information which they put together.

We are in an area of speculation here. We don't have the models against which to make our tests and on the basis of which we can have our discussion.

We've had a lot of noise with very little information, macroeconomically or microeconomically, as to what happens in industries, what happens in business and investor choices as the tax system now operates, and what might happen in other areas that we've been talking about. We don't know.

This is perhaps the first attack we ought to make. This is the pitch we made in the American Bar Committee, that we needed half a million dollars with a topflight group of economic investigators and tax practitioners who would constitute a core group that would spend full time on this effort. We need the major study, the kind of thing the Canadians got at. We need to do that and should have done it long before the Canadians showed us the way.

GEORGE J. LEIBOWITZ, Library of Congress: I'd like to raise a point of rationality. It seems to me, Dean Galvin, that your argument is bottomed on an assumption that if you had a less progressive rate structure you would have less incentive to find loopholes and other ways of avoiding the high rate.

DEAN GALVIN: Yes, sir.

MR. LEIBOWITZ: So I would like to ask this question. It seems to me that that may be putting the cart before the horse. We had a rate deduction from 90 percent to 70 percent. Did this lessen the search for loopholes and ways to avoid it? If it did not, how can we continue to assume that if we reduced it a little bit more we would then achieve the results?

DEAN GALVIN: Did it lessen the search? You gentlemen from the congressional committees and the Treasury staff can answer that better than I can. I suppose, if the rate had continued at 90 percent, we would have had a greater search for new loopholes, because, as it dropped back, there were 21 percentage points of differential. Supposedly, it becomes 21 percentage points less worthwhile to seek loopholes. But who can tell? Who knows? Does anyone?

I have no answer for that, whether or not the search for relief is less. But I know this, that we do know that the relief provisions which have been introduced in the code through the years when we had these high rates have ameliorated the effect of those rates.

If 90 percent drops down to 50 percent, I'll bet we would find less effort before the Ways and Means Committee for relief provisions. If it dropped down to 40 percent, there would be less effort. However, from 90 percent to 70 percent and for the period of time we've had it, 1964 to 1969, I don't know. These things have a lag effect.

PROFESSOR BITTKER: The difference between the possible reduction of tax by tax avoidance devices and the cost, even given the high fees of lawyers and accountants, is very substantial.

DR. NUTTER: As a general proposition of economics the demand curve slopes downward anyhow and I think we can predict that the reduction in the rates will have an effect.

WILLIAM F. HELLMUTH, formerly with Treasury Department: I would refer to the experience of 1968 when in the Revenue and Expenditure Control

Act we did get, allowing for some gimmicks, a $3 billion or $4 billion effective reduction in expenditures. But I don't think there was any single tax credit that we cut back during this period.

I don't think it's a question of the difference between night and day but perhaps the difference between 75 percent and 25 percent. Maybe the effect of recent efforts of the Treasury to publicize some of these has been to lead to the result that in the future tax credits will be more closely examined and more consistently looked at as though they were items on which there had to be annual expenditure vouchers.

PROFESSOR BITTKER: If that is so, Mr. Hellmuth, it certainly would reduce one of the arguments against using tax concessions instead of expenditures, wouldn't it? That is to say, the "burial" argument would be greatly diminished if the trend that you are describing continues.

DEAN GALVIN: Don't let him lead you into that. (Laughter.)

FRANK GRAY, Lybrand, Ross Brothers and Montgomery: I think it is worthy of accountants to indicate that considerable effort of some practitioners, and I think Mr. Bittker is one of them, has been devoted to postponing, if not avoiding, tax capital gains rates which I believe is taxed at a maximum of 25 percent or one-half of the ordinary rate, such as in corporate reorganizations and estate and gift-tax planning. Does this shed any light on your problem about the effort that will be directed to tax planning if this is done? (Laughter.)

PROFESSOR BITTKER: No, it reinforces my remark to Mr. Nutter that I think there is plenty of room for tax planning, even with a rate of 25 percent or below. A very large part, as a matter of fact, of the corporate tax practitioner's work is of course concerned with exactly that area.

MR. GRAY: That's at about 48 percent, 52 percent.

PROFESSOR BITTKER: No, I was thinking of the deferment of capital gains. The tax-exempt reorganizations, for example, is the classic case where the dispute is whether you pay 25 percent now or at a later time. Going back to Norm Ture's view that this is just a matter of discount; it's a very attractive discount, Norm.

MORTIMER M. CAPLIN, Caplin and Drysdale: I wish it were possible that we could define our goals a little more precisely. Boris, I assume, is for some broadening of the tax base, I suppose there would be some arguments of degree here, but he wants progression and Charlie wants, with a very broad base, a flat tax.

The major argument I've heard in terms of goals is that this would eliminate the work of accountants and lawyers and redirect their energies toward something else. (Laughter.) Each is saying that his system is better but better for what? Better for our economy? Better to stop riots in the streets? Better from the standpoint of democracy? Why is your system better than Boris' or vice versa?

DEAN GALVIN: It's better from the standpoint of the economy. Let's don't overplay this lawyer-accountant bit. (Laughter.) I'm not advancing that as any great big argument. But there are all kinds of services and choices made with respect to investment and activities of employment in our economy that could be made on economic grounds rather than on tax gamesmanship grounds. I think we'd have an optimum allocation of our intellectual and physical material resources through the low, flat tax on the broad base. To answer your question, a better economy, a higher standard of living, better utility of our resources, because choices are made by people on the basis of something more nearly approaching the free-market mechanism.

MR. CAPLIN: What if you had a slight progression? (Laughter.)

DEAN GALVIN: Slight? How slight? You're just quibbling with me about my ideas.

MR. CAPLIN: No, I want to know why a flat tax is better than a progressive tax. I'm not making an argument for either one. I'd like to hear from Boris why he thinks it's better to be progressive. Maybe he's the one who should defend that. Why should the man with this million dollars worth of income have to pay a 70 or 80 percent rate?

PROFESSOR BITTKER: Mort, I don't want to repeat what I said last week and, if I failed to persuade you, I'm sorry. My stress was on both equity in terms of what I believe to be ability to pay and measurement of sacrifice. I said that I thought these criteria, however discretionary and vague, cannot be disregarded. In the selection of one kind of tax rather than another you are inevitably making a judgment about what best measures ability to pay or imposes the fairest amount of sacrifice, and so on. I expressed my view that progression rated higher on that scale.

Secondly, the economic-inequality issue, which I referred to, particularly if taken in the context of government expenditures, as I would view their impact, also leads me in that direction. Mr. Edwards may be right that the uncommitted people in the middle haven't been moved by our arguments. I guess he meant *a fortiori* that those on the edges aren't swayed, but this brings me to the point at which I began last time: There is a limit to the extent to which one can get logically-satisfying or empirically-supported conclusions in this area.

I don't in the least disagree with the suggestions of Mr. Edwards and Dean Galvin that it would be useful to get a lot more information. But I don't have the slightest faith that in the end these reams of information will help us very much in making the ultimate judgment about where the burden should be placed. One's judgment of that rests upon everything that goes to make him a political and social animal. Nothing said in the course of an hour is going to alter that mix of personal characteristics very much.

MR. CAPLIN: But that's essentially the point.

PROFESSOR BITTKER: Yes.

MR. CAPLIN: That we are really talking sociology here and our own views on society.

PROFESSOR BITTKER: Yes.

MR. CAPLIN: Rather than, you know, a tax system per se. Charlie is saying it is better for our economy to have a flat system and you say your own instincts on fairness and ability to pay outweigh that. You think the economy is probably better under your system.

PROFESSOR BITTKER: I don't say it's better but I don't see it suffering so terribly, that's all.

DR. TURE: But Mort, that is not really so because what Boris has just said does not argue for a graduated rate structure. It just argues for graduated effective rates, which could be consonant with dozens of rate structures. Charles two weeks ago conceded, and he did it again tonight, that he is not really absolutely opposed to graduated effective rates, he just wants a flat rate structure. There is much more meeting of the minds between these two gentlemen than they are willing to concede. (Laughter.)

# FOOTNOTES

## FIRST LECTURE

[1] Boris I. Bittker, "A 'Comprehensive Tax Base' as a Goal of Income Tax Reform," 81 *Harvard Law Review*, 1967, p. 925; Richard A. Musgrave, "In Defense of an Income Concept," 81 *Harvard Law Review*, 1968, p. 44; Joseph A. Pechman, "Comprehensive Income Taxation: A Comment," 81 *Harvard Law Review*, 1968, p. 63; Charles O. Galvin, "More on Boris Bittker and the Comprehensive Tax Base: The Practicalities of Tax Reform and the ABA's CSTR," 81 *Harvard Law Review*, 1968, p. 1016, reprinted with additional comments in Boris I. Bittker, Charles O. Galvin, Richard A. Musgrave, and Joseph A. Pechman, *A Comprehensive Income Tax Base? A Debate* (Branford, Conn.: Federal Tax Press, Inc., 1968).

[2] *Report of the Royal Commission on Taxation* (Canada, 1966).

[3] *Economic Report of the President* (Washington: U.S. Government Printing Office, 1969), p. 241.

[4] *Ibid.*, p. 243.

[5] *The Budget of the United States Government for 1970* (Washington: U.S. Government Printing Office, 1969), p. 13.

[6] American Bar Foundation and Southern Methodist University, *Studies in Substantive Tax Reform* (Chicago: American Bar Foundation, 1969).

[7] See Robert M. Haig, "The Concept of Income—Economics and Legal Aspects," in *The Federal Income Tax*, Robert M. Haig, ed. (New York: Columbia University Press, 1921), p. 7; Henry C. Simons, *Personal Income Taxation* (Chicago: University of Chicago Press, 1938), pp. 61-62, 206.

[8] *Supra*, note 6.

[9] See House Committee on Ways and Means and Senate Committee on Finance, *Tax Reform Studies and Proposals*, U.S. Treasury Department, 1969, p. 71.

[10] Internal Revenue Service, *Individual Income Tax Returns*, 1968, p. 6.

[11] *Ibid.*

[12] *Ibid.*, p. 9.

[13] One of the best critical analyses of the case for progressivity is Walter J. Blum and Harry Kalven, "The Uneasy Case for Progressive Taxation," 19 *University of Chicago Law Review*, 1952, p. 417.

[14] See Christopher Green, *Negative Taxes and the Poverty Problem* (Washington: The Brookings Institution, 1967).

[15] Louis Eisenstein, *The Ideologies of Taxation* (New York: Ronald Press, 1961), pp. 227-28.

## SECOND LECTURE

[1] Walter J. Blum and Harry Kalven, Jr., *The Uneasy Case for Progressive Taxation* (Chicago: University of Chicago Press, 1953), reprinted from 19 *University of Chicago Law Review*, 1952, p. 417.

[2] *Ibid.*, pp. 2-3.

[3] *Ibid.*, pp. 103-04.

[4] Book review, 21 *University of Chicago Law Review,* 1954, p. 502.

[5] Book review, 67 *Harvard Law Review,* 1954, pp. 725, 730.

[6] Dan T. Smith, "High Progressive Tax Rates: Inequity and Immorality?" 20 *University of Florida Law Review,* 1968, pp. 451, 452. See also Roy Blough's review of Blum and Kalven, 56 *Columbia Law Review,* 1956, pp. 809, 811:

> In the phenomenon of progression we seem to have an example of a community judgment that originated in observation and experience and is not likely to be affected much by arguments resting mainly on deductive logic.

[7] *Supra,* note 1, p. 45.

[8] Friedrich A. Hayek, "Progressive Taxation Reconsidered," in Sennholz, ed., *On Freedom and Free Enterprise* (Princeton: Van Nostrand, 1956), pp. 265, 269-70.

[9] See the conclusion of Henry Simons, in *Personal Income Taxation* (Chicago: University of Chicago Press, 1938), p. 7:

> One derives practical implications from the criterion of equality, or proportionality, of sacrifice precisely in proportion to one's knowledge of something which no one ever has known, or ever will know, anything about. Perhaps this goes far toward explaining the popularity of these doctrines among academic writers.

[10] *Supra,* note 1, p. 104.

[11] Although Blum and Kalven reject "ability to pay" as a valid rationale for progression, they argue (*supra,* note 1, p. 64) that it is an adequate ground for choosing income, rather than some other taxable base:

> This is simply a way of saying that a tax on income is better than a tax on any less inclusive base, such as property or particular items of consumption, inasmuch as it is a better index of dollars accessible for taxes.

I do not follow this reasoning. If "accessible for taxes" means only that people with income have cash with which to pay their taxes, it is equally true that people who own property or who buy goods have "dollars accessible for taxes"; whether the tax is based on income, property, or expenditures, it will be necessary to exempt those who do not have enough to pay the tax and also provide themselves with food, shelter, and clothing; while for those above the survival level, the dollars are "accessible" no matter what the base.

[12] *Supra,* note 8.

[13] *Supra,* note 9, p. 219.

[14] For recent calculations, see House Committee on Ways and Means and Senate Committee on Finance, *Tax Reform Studies and Proposals,* U. S. Treasury Department, 1969, Part 1, Tables 5 and 6. For a discussion of the effect of taking